OF REALITY

GIANNI VATTIMO

[TRANSLATED BY ROBERT T. VALGENTI]

OF REALITY

THE PURPOSES OF PHILOSOPHY

COLUMBIA UNIVERSITY PRESS | NEW YORK

Columbia University Press
Publishers Since 1893
New York   Chichester, West Sussex
cup.columbia.edu
Della realtà © 2012 Garzanti
English translation copyright © 2016 Columbia University Press

The translation of this work has been funded by SEPS
Segretariato Europeo per le Pubblicazioni Scientifiche

Via Val d'Aposa 7 — 40123 Bologna — Italy
seps@seps.it — www.seps.it

Library of Congress Cataloging-in-Publication Data
Vattimo, Gianni, 1936–
    [Della realtà. English]
    Of reality : the purposes of philosophy / Gianni Vattimo; translated by
Robert T. Valgenti.
        pages cm
    "The Gifford lectures."
    Includes bibliographical references and index.
    ISBN 978-0-231-16696-6 (cloth : alk. paper)—ISBN 978-0-231-53657-8 (e-book)
    1. Philosophy, Modern.   I. Title.
    B794.V3813 2016
    110—dc23

                                                          2015016428

Cover and book design: Lisa Hamm
Cover image: Ben McLaughlin (contemporary artist)/Private Collection/
Wilson Stephens Fine Art, London / Bridgeman Images

For Sergio Mamino, in memoriam

Magnifice fecit Dominus nobiscum.

—PSALM 125

CONTENTS

OF REALITY

INTRODUCTION

This book, gathered around the two nuclei of lectures delivered at Leuven (1998) and Glasgow (Gifford Lectures, 2010), presents a long and rather unsystematic work of reflection on the theme of the dissolution of objectivity or of reality itself, which began with the first expressions of "weak thought" in the early 1980s. These lectures, aside from the relatively systematic intention that inspired them—the idea of presenting the meaning and results of my work to a larger philosophical audience and in more serious circumstances (in Leuven, in the Cardinal Mercier chair, where Gadamer years before had presented the core of *Truth and Method*, and also in Glasgow, in the prestigious series of Gifford Lectures)—are only a few of the stages but not their true *summae*, perhaps as they could have been. As such, they are presented here, accompanied by some essays from the same years, edited only in the conference proceedings and the lectures for which they were conceived and written. I gave up on the idea of making them into a more systematic collection, which would avoid the almost physiological repetitions that occur in such cases. The readers will judge whether this decision made sense, as I believe it did. The differing weight of certain themes—the hermeneutic *koiné* and its limits in the Leuven lectures, the temptation of realism in the Glasgow lectures—is the result of the temporal gap between the two lectures.

In Leuven I was just returning from the lectures in Bologna, also collected in *Beyond Interpretation* (1994), which had initiated the identification of hermeneutics and nihilism as the heart of weak thought; in Glasgow, however, the adversary to combat then (and today more than ever) seemed to be the return to order that was felt in the culture, not only philosophical, during these most recent years—the effect perhaps of September 11? Or of the war against international terrorism? Or of the financial crisis that it seemed could only be defeated with a "new realism" that involved paying one's debts, working more and with lower salaries, and tightening one's belt?

The result is neither a volume of popularized philosophy for the larger public nor just a record of a theoretical journey that speaks exclusively to "those in the know" or even only to biographers—mine or of weak thought. As one sees in the development of the chapters and in the unfolding of themes, the meaning of the itinerary that is presented here is also a paradox, as given in the complete title of the work, which I could also summarize by taking up one of the themes— that of the quotation marks—on which the Glasgow chapters dwell: from "reality" to reality. In effect, as I also tried to clarify with the addition in part 4 of some texts written during the same years, the initial aim of taking leave of "given" reality—first of all posing the problem of how reality is given (Heidegger: *Es gibt Sein—Es, das Sein, gibt*), in the direction of a consummation of objectivity as the effect of domination—concretized over time into a second form of "realism," which recognizes how difficult it is to take such a leave. If one prefers, the itinerary alluded to here also addresses the notion of postmodernity, which not surprisingly, from the beginning, its critics have branded as the ideology dangerously close to the illusions of triumphant neocapitalism. These criticisms, though too often inspired by a "modernism" that I continue to believe is dogmatically rationalistic (for instance, as Habermas seems to be), undoubtedly have their reasons. If I must identify a turning point, a moment of crisis or of rethinking what matters, I would point to the second edition of *The Transparent Society* (2000) and its final chapter on "the limits of derealization." As the larger part of the philosophical work—if I can say that—that began with my first book on Aristotle (at that time it was important to me to find a Christian thinking that was neither purely regressive—classic metaphysics and so on—nor dominated by a purely "liberal" modernity; it was the path of "catho-communism" that I have never left), even this turn beyond postmodernism was ethico-politically motivated, or, if one wants, "impurely" ideological; it was responding to events other than those internal to philosophical thinking; it was inspired by, or reacting to, the new situation in Italy (and in Europe) determined by the electoral victory of movements and personalities born and raised with the coming to power of various media—above all television. The possibility that the burden of "objectivity" would be alleviated almost naturally (in the end, due to technology) by the triumph of images (if you have only one television at home it functions as the source of truth; but if you have twenty of them you are more free, like Nietzsche's overman, who chooses the proper interpretation) is increasingly revealed to be an *ausgeträumt* dream, a lost illusion. Parallel to these "external events"— politics, mass society, and its ever-more visible defects—the recurring polemic against Heidegger's political choices during the years of Nazi rule represented another "realistic" motive that had to be considered with greater weight even on the theoretical level.[1] I was not satisfied with Rorty's response to Farías and his companions: by choosing to stand with Hitler in 1933, Heidegger behaved like a *son of a bitch* and made a condemnable moral choice; but what if Einstein had accepted the fascist party card? It would not have affected the validity of his theory in any way. Heidegger's Nazism and the discussions sustained by books like the one by Farías are an event that held a double significance for the question of realism: on the one side, it referred to the reality within which philosophical theories stand and to which they cannot avoid being held accountable; and on the other, it seemed to me also to deny Rorty's pacifying position, according to which one was able to distinguish between the validity of a philosophy and the morally reprehensible choices of its author. Moreover, Rorty conceived of philosophy as a "redescription" that held more or less the "validity" of a novel and was ultimately only an interpretation. But to me it seemed that neither philosophy nor perhaps even science itself was an objective form of knowledge of the "reality" out there, one that could be separated from the existential approach of the philosopher or of the scientist. Therefore, realism takes the political situation of the philosopher seriously, while antirealism admits that philosophy can be valid as a theory independently of the existential choices of the author.

The result of these two lines of reflection—which certainly now appear to me more homogenous than they might have at that time—was, on the one side, the loss of the "technological" illusion about the liberating capacity of the triumph of images, which were supposed to lighten the incontrovertability of the "real"; on the other side, the confirmation of the constant conviction that philosophy should not avoid involving itself in historical battles, even at the cost of horrible errors: I was thinking, for example, that the great thinkers of the 1920s and 1930s—except for a man like Cassirer, rich promoter of the elite German Jew, almost naturally liberal and moderate—were generally marshaled up for causes: for every Nazi like Heidegger there were Stalinists like Lukács and Bloch. Think about the famous seminar of 1930 held in Davos, where Cassirer the neo-Kantian faced off against Heidegger the existentialist (and not yet Nazi), inhabitant of the Black Forest and ultimately representative of the German proletariat that was ruined by inflation and longed for some type of redemption. There is no sympathy for Heidegger's choice to be a Nazi, obviously. But there is a complete understanding of his decision to stand up. Even in the name of an erroneous self-interpretation. Heidegger was right to think of the situation of his epoch as a clash between powers, all of which were dominated by the frenzy of technics, in versions either capitalistic or "communistic." And yet, by yielding to a late-classicist and preromantic mythology, he believed that Germany, precisely for its relative backwardness (which was such to the end of the eighteenth century and certainly much less evident in the twentieth century), might represent the site of a new pre-Socratic and premetaphysical Greece (as in the dreams of the young Nietzsche), and therefore also the alternative to the civilization of calculation, of rationalization, of *totale Verwaltung*, which the Frankfurt school was also discussing. (Moreover, what had then already struck me in Adorno was his clear conviction that Nazism was not over, that it would only be reincarnated in the mass society of America. A position that was ultimately not too far from Heidegger's.)

Certainly, I took a liking to Heidegger primarily for his anti-Americanism; and for this very reason he seems to me close to the Left, to the Frankfurt School. I am also faithful to the "avant-garde" inspiration of the Heidegger from the 1910s—an inspiration that, as one also sees in some of the pages of the text published here, also remains the point of reference for any "internal" critique of Heideggerianism, in whose name I defend the legitimacy of a "leftist" reading of his thought. (I speak of Right and Left first of all by analogy with the events of the Hegelian school, but not without a specific allusion to the current political significance of the terms.)

It might well be that the emphasis I placed on the Heideggerian decision to get involved in politics, even as we know the complete failure that resulted, was a form of defense *pro domo mea*, since in the meantime I was in my own way always wrapped up in political commitments—which I continue to believe have greater moral validity than Heidegger's, and which I hope are not a total failure (even if here there are many doubts). Commitments that I do not interpret, even in the remotest sense, as "pacifying" in the way that I view Rorty's judgment of Heidegger's Nazism. I am not a "scientist" who, having won the esteem of his fellow citizens due to the results of his work, dedicates himself to the service of the community by standing for election. In any case, my place in politics as parliamentarian and a member (independent, however) of a party with which I share goals and initiatives has further compelled me to measure myself against reality: with quotation marks or not? Right here is the problem of the quotation marks, in the sense that what really matters, and causes problems for both the philosopher and the politician (and, ultimately, for anyone who lives in a society), is the leap that those very quotation marks entail and demand. A leap signifies decision, break, and often conflict. A clash with reality, however, that is other than dissolution, the triumph of the image, the peaceful end to the incontrovertability of the given. The quotation marks are more resilient than one might expect. But the goal, the end at which they aim is still always this: to liquidate reality with those quotation marks, the simple naturalness and definitiveness of what is, of the "given," by beginning to discover what it is that gives. *Es, das Sein, gibt.* So for Heidegger, what gives in the (self-)giving [*dar(si)*] of reality is Being. Only that Being is not the God of the metaphysical tradition, and moreover not even the God of the Gospels is something of this kind. Being is not that which there is (and cannot not be), but is event, that which "gives itself" [*si dà*].[2] The Christian God is not even that which is and to which I stand in a position of pure passive contemplation; if it is, Grace actively involves the one who receives it. The self-giving of Being is certainly also a gift. But if it must not be thought as *ob-jectum*, that which I stand against and which imposes itself on me, it can only happen as an event in which I am involved and to whose determination I contribute. Interpretation, and not reflection, is what hermeneutics and Heidegger's existential analytic in *Being and Time* highlighted— not "revealed" like something to look at and notice. The novelty here, albeit relative, is the emphasis on the emancipatory meaning of hermeneutics, as one will see more clearly in the various chapters of this book, and in the passage from the Leuven lectures to those in Glasgow. Not only the hermeneutic *koiné*, namely, the more or less general admission that the experience of truth is a matter of interpretation, but the radicalization of the involvement of that very interpreter in the process (and this too is an interpretation, according to the clause in Nietzsche's maxim, assumed as a guide) and therefore in the history of Being as a process that can only be interpreted as the progressive dissolution of objectivity. A radically thought hermeneutics can only be nihilistic, namely, weak thought—the exercise of interpretation legitimated by the "fact" that Being does not give itself (any longer) as objectivity. Is it a "fact"? Yes, but in the literal meaning of the word, a meaning in the sense of Vico, we could say. The history (of Being) within which we find ourselves thrown is the history of nihilism, that is, of metaphysics and its progressive dissolution, eloquently narrated by Nietzsche and taken up again by Heidegger—a history that we cannot think from an external view (one should not forget the origins of hermeneutics and the inheritance of Dilthey, so decisive for Heidegger), as we belong to it and construct it by speaking about it.

It is not strange (to me) that, at a certain point in this itinerary, hermeneutics is always more clearly configured as a, or the, philosophy of praxis, the term that Gramsci used to indicate the thinking of Marx. As I suggested in one of the essays contained in part 4 of this book, that thinking was still exposed to the risk of ending up in metaphysical fundamentalism, to the degree that (and if really) it was thinking in terms of a truth that would refute ideologies and forms of false consciousness. What Marx and Marxism called the critique of ideology, Heidegger conceived and practiced as the critique of metaphysics, namely, the critique of the definitive claim to truth. In Marx, the reason behind ideology is relatively clear: privileges, the will to preserve and increase the division of classes, the rule of one human over another. And in Heidegger? How is metaphysics born?

In Heidegger there is no pretense of returning to the origins, moreover, by thinking of them as authentic structures because they are originary (even though in Marx there remains a sort of faith in an initial equality, broken by the originary accumulation and so on). The "always already" that Heidegger repeats often in *Being and Time* is an expression that should be taken seriously: metaphysics is not born (even if he, precisely in connection with his Nazi "error," seems to think about a premetaphysical world, the *Frühe* of the pre-Socratics, which soon fled however).[3] We recognize it not because there is an alternative model present, but because it produces the effects of the negation of freedom that Heidegger lives with in the early twentieth-century avant-garde. Moreover, all of Heideggerian ontology is a "negative ontology," or, still better, "suspensive": we do not have any experience of Being as such, we are always already in nihilism (the history in which "nothing remains of Being as such"): entities appear insofar as Being is concealed or suspended. But does this perhaps mean that it would be "better" if Being were to give itself as such and not allow entities to appear? It is clear that this question makes no sense. Not forgetting Being by allowing entities to take its place only means suspending the entity's claim to incontrovertibility.

In this "leftist" reading of Heidegger there is a good deal of Christian heritage, his and mine: the idea of a *parousia* that allows history to subsist precisely as it is suspended and that nevertheless gives it orientation and meaning. But I believe there is more, here too with some similarity between Heidegger and his interpreter. After his Nazi misadventure, as we know, Heidegger developed his reflection almost exclusively through a meditation on poetry and on the epochal words of the premetaphysical *Frühe*, in terms often so gilded that his message was barely understandable (a habit of the hermetic and oracular style that a certain type of philosophy believes it must imitate, most often with horrible results). In the end, he touched politics up close, endured a horrible burn, and thus seemed to realize the impossibility of imagining any historical order after the dissolution of the metaphysics of presence. As for his (modest?) interpreter, the analogy consists in this: the fortunes and misfortunes of the Left, in Italy and in Europe, seem understandable, at least philosophically, or, if one prefers, religiously, as a call to anarchy that is not suited to formulation in definite historical-political programs. Perhaps we can speak of reformism *vs.* revolution. It can seem like a presumptuous exaggeration, but it is not far-fetched to read the events of the Italian and European political Left also in the terms of the Sartre of the *Critique of Dialectical Reason* (1960): up to now every claim to power from the Left has always led to a "fall back into the practico-inert," a return to order—proprietary, financial,

Atlantic. We know that these failed results of what has over time appeared to us as "revolution"—from the Soviet one to the Chinese, and also, *si licet*, to our experiences of reforms, up to the very projects of the European Union, which from the beginning has seemed the way to realize socialism with a human face—are not signs of an essential human incapacity to construct a better society; we could also point to the historical forces (the "reaction lying in wait") that have over time led these experiments to failure. And nevertheless it is almost fate that the recurrence of such failures is also interpreted as a sign of something essential. The idea of anarchy with which I conclude the Glasgow lectures, one that takes up and generalizes the meaning of an important book about Heidegger by a philosopher who left us far too early (Schürmann),[4] is not a profession of metaphysical faith; it is only the result of a meditation on the praxis possible here and now, yet also a sort of "application" of Heidegger's negative ontology. The "political" perspective that has opened up since hermeneutic ontology and Heideggerian nihilism is not the sort of project one promptly takes up with the "positive" conviction of builders: as Benjamin says in the "Theses on the History of Philosophy," what inspires revolutionaries is not so much the vision of a happy world that they will construct for their descendants, but rather the image of their enslaved ancestors. The spirit of revenge? No, but the awareness that the self-giving of Being still always implies a project and thus a will to change, to conflict. And ultimately, to life.

THE LEUVEN LECTURES

THE NIETZSCHE EFFECT

I f I propose to set forth a series of philosophical reflections on the theme of (the end of) reality, it is because I believe—I feel, I have the impression that to me does not seem unfounded—that in the very relation to certain outcomes of philosophy today, outcomes that are neither marginal nor simply academic, one feels a certain *Notschrei*: if not a scream, at least an exclamation of impatience, a sort of wide-spread desire for realism (or, it seems to me, a temptation to realism). In the original presentation of these lectures at the Cardinal Mercier chair in Leuven, the various meanings that I attached to the title "De la réalité," "de realitate" in Latin, allude to this condition; of reality, please; from reality toward. . . . In opposition to the nihilistic ends of hermeneutics, which moreover I believe are implicit in the great part of today's philosophical orientations, a question regarding reality makes itself heard. I therefore speak of reality because in this way I also believe I am responding to a widespread question. This is, among other things, the only way in which philosophy can "ground itself on experience," as it has often claimed to do by believing it must refer itself to the most elemental "data" of sensations. The experience to which philosophy has to respond, and correspond, is only the question by which it feels— with all of the imprecision it implies, no less imprecise than the "pure" experience of the empiricists—questioned.

It does not seem to me that the nihilistic outcomes of hermeneutics are simply a misunderstanding to be cleared up. On the contrary, I am convinced that precisely as it is oriented to these outcomes, hermeneutics is the philosophy of our epoch—in the double sense, subjective and objective, of the genitive. Therefore I do not at all intend to respond to the need of realism by "liberating" hermeneutics from the accusation, or the suspicion, of nihilism. I am not proposing any return to reality—to foundations, to the solidity of an ontology that has its feet on the ground—against the risks of rampant irrationalism, as it seems to me is happening today in certain returns to phenomenology, now combined with the attention of the cognitive sciences, and with the interest for a Levinasian ethics and teleology,[1] or in that "tragic thought" that puts together the negative dialectics of the Frankfurt School with a reading of Heidegger as an apophantic theologian,[2] or finally in the neo-Kantianism of an Apel or Habermas. Instead, I am thinking of a movement of taking leave, of distance, of the dissolution and weakening of reality, which I see taking shape in diverse aspects of contemporary culture and which in my opinion philosophy can try to interpret only by taking it to emancipatory outcomes. I will not therefore speak against the nihilism of thinking and of culture today, but instead in favor of its more explicit assumption as a vocation (also in the religious sense) of our epoch and as a specific *chance* for emancipation.

The first step I suggest taking is placed, as the title says, under the sign of Nietzsche. Nietzsche is evoked here not as an "object" of philosophical historiography, with all of the problems that his texts continue to create for historians. Without exaggerating the meaning of this reference to Heideggerian terminology, I will say that I want to read Nietzsche in a way that is not *historisch*, but *geschichtlich*, and in the final analysis, *geschicklich*. Where, as perhaps it is worth remembering, the *historisch* reading would be precisely one directed to a philological verification of the meaning of the Nietzschean text, a verification that to the eyes of hermeneutics appears at least problematic when it is not directed by a historical purpose in the active sense (in the sense of the *res gesta*, or *gerenda*: what I am looking for in Nietzsche and why), which cannot be developed authentically (at least with the required gravity) if not by also gathering an aspect of destiny (*Geschick*). In other terms, I know well that there are a number of open philological problems regarding the meaning of Nietzsche's works, and here I do not intend to commit myself to carrying on a detailed discussion about why this meaning is necessarily the one that I find there.[3] If one prefers, what I intend to do is freely "make use" of some Nietzschean texts in order to interpret our (my?) present situation and, in a circular way, make use of this reading of the situation in order to interpret those texts. In so doing, I also believe I am conforming to the explicit ambition of Nietzsche, who wanted to be the prophet of the next century. It is due to the fact that these prophecies can be understood only gradually that, in some measure, they are realized. Let us add that Nietzsche felt himself a prophet also as *Fuersprecher*, advocate and spokesman, of a process, the eternal return of the same, that according to him was always already underway. As I hope to show more clearly in the remainder, the fact of speaking in name only of that which has already happened is another specific characteristic of the nihilistic ontology into which hermeneutics ought to flow explicitly and coherently.

But, first of all, why, and in what sense, must hermeneutics flow into an explicitly nihilistic ontology?[4] What is required, albeit paradoxically, by the contradiction that Nietzsche himself noted in the famous fragment of his posthumous notebooks: "There are no facts, only interpretations," to which he added, "And this too is an interpretation"?[5] If the hermeneutics of today is not completed in a nihilistic ontology, it forgets exactly this decisive conclusion and exposes itself to the deserved accusation of a performative self-contradiction that realists have always believed could bring an end to nihilism, just as happened with skepticism.

If the thesis of a more radical hermeneutics (but also, simply, more coherent, at least to the degree to which it is not reduced to a technical discipline, to the art of exegesis) can be summarized by this passage from Nietzsche, it is clear that the claim could not be put forward as the description of a fact, as a metaphysical proposition about reality that would be constituted "objectively" by interpretations and not by facts. First of all, it seems undeniable that hermeneutics broadly construed as philosophy—in the sense that it has acquired at least since Heidegger and Gadamer—can only be formulated in that Nietzschean maxim. It is not at all obvious, but rather highly up for debate, that Gadamer's famous claim from *Truth and Method* "*Sein, das verstanden werden kann, ist Sprache*" ("Being, that can be understood, is language") only regards that type of Being that can be understood, namely, the object of the "human sciences" (we could say, symbolic forms, the formations of the human spirit as texts, institutions, and so on).[6] Gadamer has never explicitly endorsed a radically nihilistic interpretation of this maxim or, in general, hermeneutic ontology;[7] but the whole of his thinking at least authorizes such an interpretation, to the degree that one can certainly not attribute to it a Kantian or Diltheyian sort of attitude, which would separate the realm of interpretative understanding, of *Verstehen*, from the realm of explanation in the experimental sciences. Gadamer is right to want to maintain some difference between the language of the positive sciences and the language of the human sciences (which according to him is more directly connected to everyday language).[8] But it remains true that according to him any experience is possible only within the horizon of language, and therefore of understanding. Experience, every type of experience, is possible because we "are in dialogue,"[9] because we inherit a natural language that constitutes our fore-understanding of the world. Of the world, let us emphasize, and not of Being, since it would be impossible to think that fore-understanding is something prior to Being. Being—of the world and of ourselves— gives itself only in understanding (and) in language. The thesis according to which "Being, that can be understood, is language" cannot therefore be applied exclusively to the realm of the human sciences. If experience is possible only on the basis of a previous opening, which according to Heidegger and Gadamer is that of language, it must be said that every "fact" is the product of an interpretation.

Even though this conclusion is not found explicitly in Gadamer's work, one can say that after him and after Heidegger the Diltheyan distinction between the natural sciences and the human sciences, which also (and perhaps necessarily in that conceptual picture) implied the methodological superiority of the former (since the law-giving model of science remains dominant in Dilthey, and it is likely a direct Kantian inheritance), ends up completely undermined: the natural sciences are developed only within the horizon of language that is naturally inherited with the same historical constitution of our being-in-the-world, namely, within that prior opening that conditions every experience and, therefore, constitutes its unavoidably interpretative character.

Interpretation means this very thing in *Being and Time*: to be able to access the world by virtue of a fore-understanding that constitutes us and that is identified with the inheritance of our historical-natural language. One could say that we are not very far from Kant, with the difference here that the Kantian belief in the "natural" stability of the a priori is completely dissolved. As one knows, for Kant every experience of things is made possible by an "equipping" that the subject has naturally at its disposal: all finite rational beings experience the world in the a priori forms of time and space, they order it according to the categories (such as substance, cause and effect, and so on) that are the same in everyone—whence the universality and "objectivity" of our judgments and knowledge. But Kant's transcendental subject is not a true subject, as Dilthey had already observed and as Husserl continually reaffirms in *The Crisis of the European Sciences*; it is only the correlate to the object of the sciences. In a certain sense, precisely insofar as experience is made possible only through the a priori that the subject has at its disposal "before" encountering the world, one can say that already in Kant there is a prelude to hermeneutics. Heideggerian *Dasein* (namely, man as existing), on the other hand, is constituted by a radically finite fore-understanding, *geworfen*, thrown into the concrete of a historically determined condition; therefore, *Dasein* is not the bearer of an always equal human reason. Let us not forget that what separates Heidegger from Kant is the birth of historical consciousness in the nineteenth century, and above all the rise of cultural anthropology, no less than the first signs of the "decline of the West" and its faith in itself as the center and criterion of every true humanism.

I will return later to the ontological implications of Heideggerian *Geworfenheit*. As for Nietzsche, one can view his thought as an interim stage on the path that leads from Kant's transcendental subject to Heidegger's historically thrown *Dasein*. This is what I wanted to highlight with the title of the first two chapters in this book: for Nietzsche, the true world has become a fable (according to another famous passage from his late period work *Twilight of the Idols*),[10] that is, in his thought the radicalization of the always finite and thrown character of understanding will now only give rise to a relativism that is limited to overturning, without really overcoming, positivist naturalism. According to the long fragment from his early writings "On Truth and Lying in a Non-Moral Sense,"[11] "consciousness" is nothing more than the effect of the creation of metaphors by a subject that for its part does not have a stable structure and that is constituted by a movable hierarchy of drives. It deals with an always subjective activity, even if Nietzsche— who remains in that a tributary of positivistic naturalism—does not refuse to point out the instinct of survival as the basis for the activity of consciousness. This basic motive does not, however, guarantee a stability comparable to that of Kantian reason. As survival, in natural conditions, depends always on the struggle between living things, the metaphors that are created by the activity of consciousness are always different and, as the early fragment still states, they are stabilized only in a provisional way, in connection with the formation of relations of domination, whether they are outside or inside the subject. There is no way of stabilizing once and for all the metaphors "most favorable" to survival, and therefore the reference to this "natural" impulse does not allow it to grant unity to any one of them. The nature of Nietzsche is no longer the nature of Kant, which was still capable of acting as a divine force that could inspire the creativity of artistic genius. It is only the stepmother nature of Schopenhauer, dominated by the struggle of all against all. Moreover, the instinct of survival is not even something insuperable and final: in his notes from the later years, Nietzsche (by returning in some sense to his early Schopenhauerianism) considers art precisely as a capacity to rise above the impulse of survival. Although in many ways still rooted in a naturalistic picture of a positivistic stamp, and even at the cost of the many contradictions that remain open to the very end, Nietzsche's perspectivism does not at all refer back to any "principle of reality."[12]

◆ ◆ ◆

These contradictions of Nietzschean philosophy, a blessing and a curse to interpreters, are also no less prophetic than the dissolution of Kantianism. In the sense that, in what I believe can be called the "hermeneutic *koinē*" of today's thought—or rather, the almost general agreement over the interpretative character of experience (and) of truth[13]—one does not in general go beyond the problematic conclusions of Nietzsche: consciousness is nothing other than interpretation; and this is also an interpretation—but such a conclusion does not give rise, except in Heidegger, to the developments that it deserves. The nihilistic ontology that is announced in Nietzsche, in these conditions, remains little more than an implicit nihilism, giving rise to relativist and irrationalist mentalities that, by reaction, stimulate the need— what I would call neurotic—for a return to "realism." In the most popular form today, the perspectivism (also) of Nietzschean inspiration is presented as a return to the pragmatism that considers as more or less insuperable the reference of multiple interpretations to the background, ultimately nonhistorical, of the instinct of survival.[14]

Even if with a certain caution, I use the term "neurotic" to connote the need to return to the realism that I feel is widespread in the contemporary mindset. Here it would be difficult to justify the use of this term in all of its amplitude and specificity, at least to the degree that it seems to return necessarily to the idea of a "normal" state, namely, yet again, to something that would act as a "principle of reality." Once more, a similar observation reveals the difficulty, from which Nietzsche himself has not fled, of avoiding the language and the attitude of "objectivistic" metaphysics. Without saying too much more on this terminological problem (which is also much more than that), I will admit that I use the adjective "neurotic" without any claim to rigor, assuming its imprecise but shared meaning, in order to point out that the roots of the need for realism are found, according to me, in a psychological discomfort rather than in a strictly conscious demand: namely, it is not in order to correspond to some real order that, in contrast to the perspectivist nihilism of Nietzsche (and most relativism today), one invokes a return to realism. In fact, even among the "realists" one often finds a complex mix of "foundational" arguments (the defense of the "objective" weight of perceptions, of the unavoidable passivity of sensible intuition, and so on) and ad hominem, rhetorical-persuasive arguments that frequently appeal to the unacceptable consequences of hermeneutic nihilism, which would open the way to the dissolution of every morality (if God is dead, anything goes) and, above all, to a dangerous devaluation of the experimental sciences. A similar mix of descriptive arguments and historical-moral arguments is at times also found among hermeneutic thinkers: even Gadamer's *Truth and Method* can appear as a defense of the interpretative character of experience, founded, however, on the "objective" phenomenological description of its authentic structures. The same holds, naturally, for the existential analytic of *Being and Time*, which nevertheless, in the development of Heideggerian thought, is revealed always more clearly as the ladder that one must allow to fall away once one has scaled the haystack.

We are once again faced with the performative contradiction, apparent or real, that Nietzsche explicates at the end of his maxim: "And this too is an interpretation." What happens—not in Heidegger, certainly, and only apparently in Gadamer, but for sure in the greater part of today's hermeneutic *koiné*—is that one assumes, more or less consciously, the maxim from Nietzsche (there are no facts, only interpretations) as a description of the state of things, and thus as a metaphysical thesis. Can we see here a confirmation of the difficulty—on which Heidegger never stopped meditating—that thought encounters when it searches for a way beyond metaphysical objectivism? Even for those who admit that consciousness is interpretation, namely, access to the world with the mediation of a fore-understanding, it is difficult to get used to the idea that there are only ad hominem arguments, only interpretations that are risky, liable (but not necessarily unreasonable), historically situated, and inevitably "interested"—especially in a field like philosophy, which is never a "normal science" in the Kuhnian sense of the term.[15]

The timeliness of Nietzsche's nihilistic perspectivism—which not surprisingly is the subject of the last chapter of Habermas's *Knowledge and Human Interests*, a book that can be considered a sort of introduction (however polemical) to the hermeneutic *koiné* of today—can be easily documented in a text, more recent than Habermas's and of an "analytic" origin, such as John McDowell's *Mind and World* from 1994.[16] This text is extremely important not only for the clarity and the rigor of its exposition, but above all because, in my view, it shows (a) the legitimacy of a hermeneutics of the Nietzschean sort even for an "analytic" sensibility such as the author's, and (b) the persistence of a metaphysical-descriptive prejudice that keeps one from following out to their completion (and, according to me, with Heidegger) the implications of the truth of hermeneutics for philosophy itself ("and this too is an interpretation").

McDowell finds that the relation between mind and world tends to be presented—in the authors he examines and discusses, on the one side Donald Davidson, and on the other Gareth Evans, moreover assumed as emblematic of widely shared theoretical attitudes—as an oscillation between two contrary poles, one attributable to Davidson's "coherentism" and the other that takes refuge in what, with Sellars,

McDowell calls "the Myth of the Given": "We are prone to fall into an intolerable oscillation: in one phase we are drawn to a coherentism that cannot make sense of the bearing of thought on objective reality, and in the other phase we recoil into an appeal to the Given, which turns out to be useless."[17] The "intolerable" character of oscillation is neither discussed nor explained further in this place (perhaps even here one could speak of "neurotic"?). In order to understand why coherentism might not be preferable in itself, one needs to take into account the reasons that McDowell presents in the preceding pages of the book, which can be summarized as such: coherentism does not do justice to the experience of the nonarbitrariness that we have in the awareness of reality. And in any case, as he shows in his discussion, Davidson's coherentism—in which a belief can be "proved" only by another belief, while sensible perception can only produce "effects"—is limited to isolating a world of causes and effects (physical, neuronal, and so on) from the world of beliefs that is independent of it. One notes that, as McDowell writes, "According to Davidson, experience is causally relevant to a subject's beliefs and judgment, but it has no bearing on their status as justified or warranted. . . . Experience cannot count as a reason for holding a belief."[18] That means that "Davidson's picture is that we cannot get outside our beliefs."[19] As for the Myth of the Given, which McDowell analyzes by examining a work of Gareth Evans,[20] according to him one takes leave of it through an overturning of the idea of concept formation by way of abstraction, which refers to Wittgenstein's observations about private language. By analyzing the reflections of Wittgenstein, in particular his notion of ostensive private definition, McDowell shows that the idea that the concept is formed by abstraction from individual experiences is rightly rejected by Wittgenstein on the basis of the principle according to which "a bare presence cannot be a ground for anything" on the level of concepts and judgments.[21] The Given is always given, in its fragmentary and punctual self-presentation, to an individual person (an observation that could be developed, differently than happens in Wittgenstein or in McDowell himself, in the

Heideggerian or Derridean direction of a more general delegitimization of presence and its presumed ontological importance). If I understand McDowell's thesis well, in order to become the foundation for propositions and judgments, the given offered by mere presence—verified in sensation and, if need be, assumed in the ostensive private definition—must be subsumed within a discursive network that can only be the result of a spontaneous activity of the subject.

Spontaneity is an explicitly Kantian term. In order to put an end to the sterile—and "intolerable"—oscillation between pure coherentism and the Myth of the Given, McDowell refers in fact to Kant, even if by interpreting him in a way that is rather unique and not free from misunderstandings. The opposition between concepts and givens, which is expressed without being mediated in the described oscillation, is in fact derived from the radical difference that separates the spontaneity of concepts from the receptivity and passivity of sensations. It is, as one will remember, the problem that Kant resolves with the doctrine of the schematism, the doctrine that McDowell, curiously, does not bring up in his discussion, except by suggesting in its place a type of "Aristotelian" surrogate. This forgetfulness likely happens more than just by chance, as it seems that McDowell understands the spontaneity of the intellect and of Kantian reason by almost completely confusing it with freedom in the sense of a faculty of choice, in such a way that, in certain passages of his text, the application of the a priori to the data of sensibility ends up appearing like the free initiative of the conscious subject. For example, one reads on page 12: "The conceptual capacities that are passively drawn into play in experience belong to a network of capacities for active thought, a network that rationally governs comprehension-seeking responses to the impacts of the world on sensibility." This "network," which takes on the function of the Kantian schematism, is not entrusted to the will of the conscious subject, nor is it even an immutable, "natural" endowment; McDowell resorts to the term "second nature," referring back to Aristotle, with the result of turning Kantianism in a Hegelian direction. The network is a sort of system of a priori forms that are nonetheless historically qualified, and McDowell thus calls it *Bildung*, culture. But it is part of "our way of realizing that we are animals," and here again the proximity with Nietzsche's perspectivism is clearly visible, even if it is only implicit. Without following out this discussion of McDowell any longer, it seems doubtful to me that also in his case, which I assumed as exemplary of perspectivism with an analytic origin, we face a naturalistic vision of the interpretative character of experience that does not mature in an engagement of nihilism precisely because, or as, it is conceived as an "external" description of "given" structures. There are no facts, only interpretations; yet, they are not arbitrary because they are supported by the logic of (second) nature and therefore, as in Nietzsche, by the logic of survival. But that this too is an interpretation remains a conclusion completely off limits.

◆ ◆ ◆

Let us summarize the meaning of this excursus for our discussion: the worrying gap that seems to persist between the spontaneity of reason and the passivity of sensibility can be overcome if one no longer thinks of nature exclusively in the deterministic terms of modern scientism; it is rightfully nature, an aspect of our nature as rational animals, the fact of living always within an environment of culture, of tradition, of *Bildung*, that for us has the sense and the importance of a second nature. The intellectual schemata that we apply to the data of sensible experience are nonarbitrary ways of interpreting the world because they conform, exactly, to this second nature that is the (dominant?) culture of our society, which, let us not forget, is not intangible, and thus develops historically. The natural character of this second nature, we could conclude, does not consist so much in its corresponding to an immutable essence of things, but rather in the fact that, *ça va sans dire*, it is identified with the naturalness of the facts conforming to expectations, to their use, and so on—a conclusion that is not explicit in

McDowell, but that seems perfectly in agreement with the whole of his argument, and whose persuasiveness, at least in view of the objectives that are presented, one can legitimately doubt. If it is in fact a matter of justifying the feeling of friction with this nonmechanistic idea of nature—a feeling that is nonetheless implicit in the experience of consciousness and that, in such a way, would render the passivity of sensible experience less irremediably heterogeneous with respect to the spontaneity of reason—what we have gained in the end is the idea that the cogency and the friction depend on the force with which the conceptual schemata of that culture into which we are thrown establish themselves in every one of our encounters with the world. What strikes our sensibility, in the literal sense of the word, as an external and intractable given is none other than the force of Hegelian objective spirit or, in Nietzschean terms, of the dominant culture, "the voice of the herd in us." A conclusion that I would not hesitate to share if he were not to stop here, if he were also not to remain entangled in the performative contradiction that the hermeneutic *koiné* of today also appears not to know how to overcome.

Even though it is a rather long way back, let us return to our Nietzschean point of departure: it does not in fact seem to me that McDowell's position—which I also find exemplary, at least in very general terms, of other similar positions, such as Rorty's neopragmatism or Putnam's "internal realism"—is far from the Nietzschean thesis according to which there are no facts, but only interpretations. What distinguishes Nietzsche's from McDowell's is solely a more explicit awareness of the always social, and thus authoritarian, character of *Bildung* and of tradition. Gadamer, by responding to the objections of Habermas,[22] has at least provided arguments capable of dispelling the suspicion of traditionalism and authoritarianism: the historical horizons within which the experience of truth is always gathered are never closed, as this too would be an arbitrary objectivist-metaphysical hardening, which gives rise precisely to the typically metaphysical mistake of relativism. The thinkers of the analytic tradition like McDowell, instead, do not seem to be aware that the naturalness of their second nature (or also the naturalness of the Rortyan world of conversation, also "naturally" preferable for reasons of survival) hides, always already, the problem of the concrete, historical coming into form of *Bildung*, with its conflicting and dominating aspects—precisely that problem of effective historicity of the same hermeneutic thinker who prevented Nietzsche from stopping at the (objective) "observation" of the interpretative character of consciousness. Moreover, in this closing off of the historical-concrete problematic of *Bildung*, the analytic thinkers do nothing but closely follow an attitude already quite present in the late Wittgenstein, whose analyses of language differ from an *Andenken* of the hermeneutic type precisely due to the absence of a historical dimension.[23]

The "naturalism" of McDowell, tempered by the reference to Aristotle, therefore seems to me exemplary of the fact that, in the end, thinkers with an analytic education who are nonetheless closer to the hermeneutic *koiné*—I am here thinking of Hilary Putnam, Nelson Goodman, the aforementioned Rorty, Bas van Fraassen, and more recently the scientific perspectivism of Ronald Giere[24]—remain stuck to an attitude similar to Nietzschean perspectivism intended as a descriptive doctrine of the "real" structures of experience. There are good reasons for believing that Nietzsche himself had not completely developed the consequences of the final observation according to which "this too is an interpretation." And yet he had a clear enough awareness of these consequences, to the degree that he did not consider himself satisfied with perspectivism understood as a descriptive doctrine of the real sate of things. This, at least, seems to me to be the meaning of one of the more important pages of *Thus Spoke Zarathustra*,[25] the one that discusses "The Convalescent" (in the third part), in which Zarathustra scolds the animals for having misunderstood the doctrine of the eternal return of the same. While they joyously sing "Everything goes, everything comes back; the wheel of being rolls eternally," Zarathustra censures them harshly because they have forgotten the effort that his work "of seven days" had cost him, in the course of which he was obliged to bite off and spit out the head of the serpent (which is covered in a preceding section, "The Vision and the Enigma"). And you, Zarathustra says, have forgotten my terrible effort and "have already made a hurdy-gurdy song of it." I do not want to get into a detailed discussion,[26] but it seems clear to me that, on the theme of the eternal return, but also on the very similar theme of perspectivism, Nietzsche is perfectly aware that his doctrine is neither the description nor the theoretical assertion of a given metaphysical structure. The head of the serpent must be bitten off in order to "institute" the eternal return. For that is the theme that occupies us here: the dissolution of reality in interpretation is also an (act of) interpretation, which puts the historicity of the interpreter into play, and is not a discovery or a shedding of light onto a past error that would be uncovered on the basis of an objective awareness of the facts. The animals of Zarathustra take the eternal return too lightly, just as if one were dealing with a show or a game. One cannot say this literally of the thinkers just alluded to moments before—they certainly do not deserve to be accused of having made hermeneutics into a hurdy-gurdy song, or of having behaved like animals, even those of Zarathustra. And yet, as I have argued at length elsewhere (for example, in *Beyond Interpretation*), the limit of the more or less explicit Nietzscheanism that circulates within the hermeneutic *koiné* of today, even in its "continental" side (I am thinking of Derrida, above all), consists precisely in its not having developed to the fullest extent the conclusion of Nietzsche's maxim—this too is an interpretation. In the parable of Zarathustra the error of the animals is not analyzed in a more precise way. But it is not difficult to read such an analysis in the other works of Nietzsche, an analysis that justifies my earlier use of the term "neurotic." Not being able, moreover like us, to explain the persistence of the need for objectivity as a "pure" theoretical need—namely, as if it were to express an originary impulse to the faithful reflection of things, independently of interests, passions, prejudices (therefore, of all of those "effects of will" that, for Descartes and for the rationalistic tradition, bring about error as they prevail wrongfully on the clarity of the intellect)—Nietzsche sides with passion over objective truth by referring to psychological or more generally anthropological motivations.

The thesis for which there are no facts but only interpretations first of all has a gnoseological meaning, which perhaps is not the most original and is founded upon the radical phenomenalism of the already cited fragment "On Truth and Lying in an Non-Moral Sense": the creation of metaphors, which makes up consciousness, is an individual activity, but, in the end, a language of truth is constructed together with the very constitution of society—the strongest impose their own language as the "normal" language, which must be used in order to understand and to speak the truth "in a non-moral sense," namely, in order to produce "true" descriptions of the reality "out there." In the idea of a "normal" metaphorical language, which reduces all of the other systems of individual metaphors to the rank of pure subjective poetical expressions, another element becomes clear for today's hermeneutic *koiné*, still more important than the purely gnoseological one: the idea that "normal" language is nothing more than a system of metaphors (even if they are in their origin purely subjective) that is imposed on the others for reasons not at all theoretical and "pure," but for practical motives and relations of domination.

This model, somewhat rough, is articulated and becomes complicated in the development of Nietzschean thought—first of all by means of a kind of extension of sociology to individual psychology. It is not in fact only society in the strict sense that violently reduces the multitude of metaphors in the bounds of a hierarchy dominated by "normal" language; even that which we call individual is in effect a *dividuum*, a multiplicity in which identity is constituted through a struggle, among diverse forces never definitively concluded, which gives rise to more or less stable configurations.[27] It is precisely here that the notion of interpretation is introduced. According to an important passage in *The Gay Science*,[28] the hierarchy that is established within the subject is determined by the same social motivations discussed in the early fragment on truth as metaphor: the same self-awareness is not at all necessary for the dividual-individual [*l'individuo-dividuo*] as such, and it is required only because it can communicate and "answer" for itself in the relation of domination. Even without exaggerating the importance of this observation, the relation between the interior hierarchy of the subject and its sociopractical needs is clear in Nietzsche. If they are not relations of domination, it will be the need for survival more generically understood that structures the *dividuum* hierarchically in a relatively stable way. In any case, in Nietzsche one cannot separate the pressure of the demands for survival from the pressure exacted by the relations of domination. It is what always becomes clearer in the writing of the later period, from *On the Genealogy of Morality* to the notes that according to an abandoned project he had thought to reunite under the title of *The Will to Power*; although, regarding this expression, it ought to be considered that power for Nietzsche is not a preeminently sociopolitical notion, as the struggle for power is also and above all a conflict of interpretations, in which no level, neither that of physical power nor that of political domination, can be considered more fundamental than the others.[29] The Nietzsche of the posthumous writings, ultimately, is neither (or is not solely) the theorist of a society of masters and slaves that regulate their relationship through a life-or-death struggle, nor the theorist of natural selection. What he says in the long fragment on European nihilism written at Lenzerheide during the summer of 1887—according to which, in the outbreak of the struggle of all against all that follows the death of God, the most violent do not win, but rather the "most moderate"—is explained exactly according to the idea that power is the imposition of an interpretation over other interpretations, and that such predominance is not necessarily established by means of physical violence. Naturally that does not exclude that the will to power, as will to interpretation, symbolic creativity, the invention of metaphors, could be in its turn intimately conditioned by the interiorized traces of domination and of violence ("the voice of conscience is the voice of the herd").[30] In the postmodern perspective that I continue to profess (even though by many it is declared *de[post]modé*), one can also reasonably think that the hermeneutic *koiné*—which, if my hypothesis has any merit, has become hegemonic in a large portion of today's culture—was made possible by the transformation of social relations in the sense of the reduction of the violence enacted by technology, of the diffusion of economic well-being, and of the establishing of democratic political regimes. As is clear, it is a bit like Herbert Marcuse's argument—unjustly forgotten today—about repressive tolerance and the possibility of emancipation that our society possesses and does not exploit radically enough. In Nietzsche, God is dead, but a good deal of time must still pass before the announcement of his death is received.[31]

All of these levels of significance that are found in the "gnoseology" of Nietzsche must here be remembered with the goal of not being deceived about the meaning of one such operation of excavation: it is not about arriving at the ultimate level, which would still function as a principle of reality. The need for realism is, ultimately, an effect of *ressentiment*, of the "tedious qualities of old dogs and men who have long been kept on the leash."[32] Rather, there are just these multiple and irreducible levels of significance that support the "prophetic" character of Nietzsche's maxim about facts and interpretations, and they constitute the permanent timeliness of it. This timeliness becomes evident to us also because, in the meantime, we have gotten to know Marx, Freud, and many other "masters of suspicion" who have marked the culture of the last century. At least it offers a guiding thread for beginning to explain the "resistance" of realism that, in today's hermeneutic *koiné*, keeps the implications of the phrase "this too is an interpretation" from their fullest development. By failing to clarify all of this phrase's historical-existential-ontological implications, Nietzsche himself left this work undeveloped, or rather, in the form of an obscure prophesy. That will be the theme of our upcoming reflections, with guidance provided by Heidegger.

2 THE HEIDEGGER EFFECT

We have evoked, at the end of the previous chapter, the "resistance" of realism, a resistance that, from the point of view of a thinking that no longer wishes to be metaphysical, can only be described as neurotic, at least in the general sense that I pointed out. Let us say that the "need for reality" is not at all a natural "ultimacy"; it is always something positive, in the sense that it arises from a cultural choice, from a historical habit that can also be called a type of "second nature," but that does not possess the intangibility and the ahistorical rigidity of the first nature. This habit blocks thought from pushing itself to the nihilistic consequences of Nietzsche's maxim, from becoming completely aware that "this too is an interpretation." The need for reality is neurotic, we could say, because it refuses to take notice of the "logical" need (it is also, besides, not at all "natural," but only an open possibility for thinking) to recognize itself as gathered within that game of interpretation that claims to be the only "reality." Here we find ourselves facing two equal possibilities, and I am aware that even though neither of them has the metaphysical cogency of "natural" essences, we risk also having to consider as neurotic the choice to develop Nietzschean nihilism logically to its extreme conclusions. And this too is "only" a decision, in the same way as the other. Are there good reasons to prefer it? The answer is articulated on various levels. First of all, there is the inevitable circularity of the hermeneutic attitude, which is "proved" only by developing its own premises, in a pragmatistic sense that hermeneutics is rather far from denying. The circularity here is recognized explicitly, and this would already be a good reason for preferring the nihilistic path over the realist one. This latter is neurotic precisely to the degree that it refuses to acknowledge its character as a practical choice, as an acquired habit. Everything goes back, as can be seen, to the fact of not wanting to recognize its involvements in the game of interpretation; in the final analysis, back to a rejection of finitude, that (and this perhaps would have to be the true "realism," not the neurotic one) involves a determinate position in the world, and thus "taking a stand." In existentialistic, Kierkegaardian terms, one could say that the very possibility of choosing between a realistic attitude and a hermeneutic one "demonstrates" that the correct one is the latter, namely, that we are in an open situation in which various possibilities are announced and where a "nature" is not imposed. We are "on board," as Pascal would say; even the choice not to choose, to take refuge in objective reality, is already a choice. To speak of taking refuge, here, is not improper: with respect to the hermeneutic admission of the opening and the choice, realism appears to be a closure that reassures and stifles at the same time.

I know well that arguments of this sort seem not at all philosophical, oscillating between the most banal psychologism and sociologism and the limits of every ad hominem argument. But we are clear: the reasons that hermeneutics can put forward to "prove" its own validity can only be of this type, even though this does not mean that one can accept just any thesis. To exit from objectivistic metaphysics also means finding oneself in the condition of having to construct a completely historical rationality—in the end, more human, once again finite and therefore always situated and never neutral, oriented in a way that depends on a decision—of the individual or of an entire culture.

As is apparent, all of these are arguments that lead back to Heidegger (also here, incidentally, not to a Heidegger who is "philological" or historiographical, but *geschichtlich* and *geschicklich*). The antirealism, to call it thus, of hermeneutics is not affirmed in the tradition of Schleiermacher or of Dilthey, but begins with *Being and Time*.[1] In this work, Heidegger proposes an analysis of existence that closely ties experience to the finite, thrown, *geworfen* project that any one of us is. Here I will recall only the major points of this analysis: being means being-in-the-world; the world is made up of things; and these, first and foremost (*zuerst und zumeist*), are given to us as equipment, as they concern us always in an originary way as either hostile or friendly, useful or damaging, and so on and never as neutral objects to which a "meaning" would be attributed only after the fact. As existing beings, therefore, we are always *bestimmt*, attuned, oriented according to preferences and dislikes, never simply-present (*vorhanden*) in the midst of objects, but actively situated and committed to actions intending to flee from certain things and to seek out certain others. This is the idea of existence as a "project." It is only within the horizon of a project that things "are given." And here arises the centrality of interpretation: the experience and consciousness of truth are an articulation of the project, of the fore-understanding that we, as existing beings, always already are.

Before examining the consequences of the Heideggerian approach to existence as project, which constitute the foundation of his ontology, let us pause for a moment to observe what seems to be a contradiction in Heidegger himself. *Being and Time* seems to present itself as the phenomenological "discovery" of the objectively projectural character of existence, which arrives at the notion of interpretation by recognizing it as a "fact." This would mean that the Heideggerian existential analytic is performed on the basis of objective evidence. Now, the analyses of *Being and Time* are certainly not arbitrary constructions or pure fantasies, but it is certain that Heidegger does not undertake them with a neutral attitude. Long before *Being and Time*, Heidegger already "knows" where he wants to arrive with his analysis of existence.

In the new and definitive edition of *Wegmarken* (published for the first time in 1967), which he prepared shortly before his death (in 1976) and which was destined for the *Gesamtausgabe*,[2] Heidegger wanted to include, beyond the lecture on "Phenomenology and Theology," even the long, unedited review of *Psychologie der Weltanschauungen* by Karl Jaspers (from 1919) that he wrote between 1919 and 1921. Without even exaggerating the "testamentary" significance of such a decision, the importance of this writing for understanding the formation of Heideggerian thought cannot be lost on anyone. For what interests us here—the analysis of existence and consciousness as the circle of fore-understanding and interpretation—the discussion of Jaspers's text is revealing. Jaspers, Heidegger recalls, wanted to study the *Psychologie der Weltanschauungen* in order to understand "what the human being is,"[3] namely, in order to construct a general psychology able to trace out the horizon of the psyche in its totality. In the preface, Jaspers also wrote that by doing this he wanted to provide "clarifications and possibilities which can serve as means to our self-reflection (in our worldviews)."[4] This latter intention, Heidegger says, is the "properly philosophical" one. Naturally, it does not assume that Jaspers judges the worldviews that he studies on the basis of an assumed systematic conception such as the "truth"; nevertheless, what he himself says about his own intention allows us to ask if he would "return radically to the original genetic motivations in this history" by verifying "whether these ideals satisfy the fundamental sense of philosophizing" or whether they have "never been appropriated in an original manner."[5] In the pages that follow, Heidegger introduced the expression *faktische Lebenserfahrung* (factical life experience), which one finds at the center of his 1920–21 lecture course *Introduction to the Phenomenology of Religious Life*.[6] The "properly philosophical" intent of Jaspers, that of putting into play the Weltanschauung itself, is not, according to Heidegger, realized in the work. Jaspers ends by forgetting it, dedicating himself instead to a panoramic, objectifying, and definitively "aesthetic" presentation,[7] of the various types of Weltanschauung. This attitude is called aesthetic not because it places itself in a perspective that is concerned with beauty and form; in fact, it is also able to have a moral inspiration. Rather, it is aesthetic because it is concerned with its own object—from the point of view that Gadamer later characterized as "aesthetic consciousness"—as an object of pure contemplation. One cannot possess the meaning of existence, Heidegger says, in a "theoretical manner [author's note: contemplative, objectifying], but rather by enacting [*Vollzug*] the 'am,' which is a way of being that belongs to the being of the 'I.'"[8] All of that shows "that this experience does not experience the 'I' as something located in a region, as an individuation of a 'universal.'" And still here, "The 'I' should be understood here as the full, concrete, and historically factical self that is accessible to itself in its historically concrete experience of itself." Concrete historicity does not at all signify here "the correlate of theoretical and objective historical observation; rather, it is both the content *and* the 'how' of the anxious concern of the self about itself." That has nothing to do with a further broadening of the dominant "historical consciousness," understood as a collection of knowledge about the past, the practical use of this information, and a critique of its surviving relics. It is not a matter, in a word, of *Historisches*, of historiography, but of history in progress that is actively in relation to its own past. Jaspers, and before him the phenomenology of Husserl, had given to philosophy the task of getting "to the things themselves." Therefore, without any presupposition. Already in the first pages of the review, Heidegger had written that "thinking without presuppositions is here intended to be taken in a philosophical sense and not in a specifically scientific sense. . . . It might just be the case that even in the directions of inquiry in which we could find access to the things themselves of philosophy lie covered over for us, and that what is thus necessary is a radical kind of deconstruction and reconstruction, i.e., a genuine confrontation with the history that we ourselves 'are.'" The destruction—or deconstruction—of something that one understands in the context of the writing, where it is no longer a matter of a "metaphysics" to be overcome, in the sense of the "second" Heidegger, but one speaks instead of the fact that the objective, panoramic, aesthetic presuppositions that ultimately assert themselves in Jaspers's book are the result of a tradition accepted without criticism, and not even consciously assumed. Because of this subjection to tradition, "we are unable to see phenomena of existence today in an authentic manner, we no longer experience the meaning of conscience and responsibility that lies in the historical itself (the historical is not merely something we have knowledge about and about which we write books; rather, we ourselves are it, and have it as a task)."

A term that recurs often in this text, and that is rarely cited due to the difficulty of translating it adequately, is *Vollzugssinn*—the sense of enactment. For example: "When, in accord with the relational sense of one's experience [*Bezugssinn*], one is directed historically to one's self, the context of this experience also has a historical nature in accord with its sense of enactment [*Vollzugssinn*]." Here Heidegger is trying to give a name to the historicity lived as the active assumption of an inheritance and, just a bit later, it will also be revealed to, and against, the phenomenology of Husserl himself (as seems apparent to me in pages 27–29).

I have dwelled a bit on these notes to Jaspers because, apart from the fact that they already contain many themes from *Being and Time* in their early form, they express an attitude that, without being "realist" or objectivistic in the current meaning of the term, is not at all inclined to the rule of *everything goes*, not even in the sense of promoting philosophy as the more or less literary redescription of the world. In these pages there is an effort at cogency, the search for a rationality that is exercised precisely by placing presuppositions into discussion, those very ones from which phenomenology wanted to free itself (and also Jaspers, in the wake of the *Wertfreiheit* of Weber) at the expense of falling back into an attitude that Heidegger later calls metaphysical— already seeing clearly its unsuitedness for philosophy.

The text of the review of Jaspers's book also responds, more or less completely, to the problem of the "good reasons" for preferring hermeneutics over "realism." Freedom can be realized only by beginning from the presuppositions that are gathered explicitly within their own lived historicity, that is, assumed in their *Vollzugssinn*. Here there is already the core of Heidegger's step away from Husserl, which risks not realizing that "experiencing in its fullest sense is to be found in its authentically factical context of enactment in the historically existing I."[9] The phenomenological *epoché* consists already here, for Heidegger, in the removal of every model of theoretical neutrality from consideration in favor of an explicit engagement of the *Vollzugssinn*. It is precisely by remaining faithful to Husserl's requirement of going to the things themselves that Heidegger, in the end, becomes unfaithful to him. But it would be imprecise to say that the emphasis placed on the *faktische Lebenserfahrung* and on *Vollzugssinn* responds to a demand with a more rigorous theoretical foundation. In these same pages we are now discussing, Heidegger leaves out that the various experiences of existence (aesthetic, moral, religious) can be described phenomenologically from the point of view of a theoretical model.

Without tackling here the illustration of the lecture course *Introduction to the Phenomenology of Religious Life* held in Freiburg during the same period in which he wrote his review of Jaspers's work, I will bring it up only to mention what seems to me one of the indisputable roots of the difference that separates Heidegger from Husserl up through the early years of the 1920s, which is undoubtedly the personal interest in theology. Moreover, Husserl would later recall it in one of his letters from 1920 by reassuring Natorp on the fact that by now his young assistant is "freed from dogmatic Catholicism."[10] Husserl came to philosophy through mathematics; Heidegger, on the other hand, from Catholic theology. If I may paraphrase a title from Ernst Bloch, the "spirit of the avant-garde" was decidedly more detectable in Heidegger. Bloch's book *The Spirit of Utopia* clearly expresses the atmosphere of the early decades of the century,[11] the revolt against the rule of exteriority, of social rationalization, in the name of existence and its open and contradictory character. This atmosphere is the same one that Heidegger would evoke, many years later, in the lecture given upon the occasion of his nomination to the Academy of Sciences in Heidelberg,[12] an atmosphere characterized by the popularity of

Dostoevsky, by the Kierkegaard renaissance, by the first dissemination of the works of Nietzsche. Bloch's philosophical expressionism, the dialectical theology of Barth, and first of all the debate between the *Naturs-* and *Geisteswissenschaften* are all testimonials to this atmosphere. In the years surrounding World War I, the process of the rationalization of social labor was greatly intensified, which later inspired Chaplin's polemic *Modern Times* as the imaginary of futurists and the catastrophic utopias of expressionistic cinema. The "existentialist" tone of the philosophical, artistic, literary, and theological culture of these years is all an effort to stand against what Adorno would later call *totale Verwaltung*—the total organization of society.

Without discussing the influence of Husserl and more generally the German philosophical tradition, one must also refer to this background in order to understand the sense and the importance of Heidegger's re-posing of the question of Being. Would it be correct to consider it just a development of the Husserlian question about regional ontologies and fundamental ontology? Already in the published sections of *Being and Time*, Heidegger rejects the metaphysical notion of truth as correspondence. At least on this basis—but always more clearly on the basis of texts like the review of Jaspers and the lectures on religion published around that time—it is impossible to attribute to him the desire to rediscover, in his research, the "objectively" true meaning of Being, which metaphysics would have forgotten and replaced with a "false" meaning. What he wanted to question, up through the early 1920s, was instead the "historical" fact of this forgetting, the same forgetting that was there at the root of the *totale Verwaltung* that was being constructed in the 1910s, and against which the avant-garde had posed its existentialistic sensibility.

The radicalization of the phenomenological call *zu den Sachen selbst*; the sensitivity to the spirit of the avant-garde and its ethical-political rather than purely theoretical motivations; the sizeable traces of the religious and theological interest that had not yet been set aside: these are the principle components that come together in the program that reproposes the problem (of the forgetting) of the meaning of Being that guides *Being and Time*. One always needs to keep this in mind, like a guiding thread for the interpretation of all of the works of Heidegger, and when, as in the case of his attachment to Nazism, it needs to be asserted against the self-interpretation of Heidegger himself.

At this point in the discussion, it seems to me that by now the reasons ought to be clear why the hermeneutics of Heidegger line up with Nietzsche's maxim "there are no facts, only interpretations." But beyond this, I believe that one begins to catch sight of the sense in which Heidegger seems to be the one thinker of the twentieth century who also takes the conclusion of Nietzsche's maxim seriously: "And this too is an interpretation." It is true that, in the texts we have now cited, Heidegger insists on the historicity of Dasein above all with the aim of removing from consideration the objectivism to which Jaspers (and in the end also Husserlian phenomenology) falls victim. What matters to us, nevertheless, is the broader meaning of the reference to *Vollzugssinn*. Though he does not yet explicitly thematize authenticity (*Eigentlichkeit*), Heidegger continually returns to the "authentic" (*eigentlich*) meaning of philosophy, which consists in taking up its own historical situation not only in terms of *Historie*, of the whole of historiographical data to be gathered and catalogued, but in an act that, instead of being limited to the objective reflection of the given, is in the fullest sense historical initiative as *res gesta*, and thus *geschichtlich*.

◆ ◆ ◆

So what comes, in Heidegger, from this attention to *Vollzugssinn* (what, said once and for all, is the "meaning that is constituted while it is recognized," which thus must more or less be understood; or even, what is present in its fulfillment in our active comprehension; ultimately, we know history and this is a new historical act)? I said that this will be called, in *Being and Time*, authenticity; as Heidegger always insists, it pertains not to a particular moral criterion of behavior (since, in the end, an authentic behavior would be "better" only because it was not "false" in the sense of correspondence, objectively corresponding to something, to myself "true"), but precisely with the nonmetaphysical opening of historicity. Things reveal themselves in their truth, Heidegger will say in *Being and Time*, only to an authentically open project. Let us clarify: this is not a matter of assuming one's own historicity in an authentic way because things would thus appear better in all of their objective truth. It is a matter of freeing them from the false light in which the objectifying conception of metaphysics places them. In order to place them where, and for what reason? The preference, surely not ethical in the sense of respect for the law, that Heidegger shows for authenticity is inspired by his will to go beyond metaphysics. As I have emphasized, this will is motivated more ethically-politically than it is descriptively: in conformity with the spirit of the avant-garde, Heidegger wants to overcome objectivism because he fears its totalizing and totalitarian capacity; this is not done, however, to achieve a greater objectivity, or to conform better to some givenness, of essences or laws. It is certain that in the language of *Being and Time*, which is still in many ways phenomenological, things allow themselves to be discovered only by an authentic project. The idle talk of the world of the "they," of *das Man*, causes entities to fall into disguise and closure. The identification with the they signifies the supremacy of the shared interpretative state.[13] Truth must be chosen: it needs *krinein logo*, judging in the *logos*.[14] Things are therefore discovered only in what is an "authentic" project, one that is qualified and "someone's." This is understood if one recognizes any of the fundamental points of the existential analytic that were developed right in the opening paragraphs of the work. We can summarize it in this way: the world is given to us as world—and that means as a whole ordered in some way, first of all according to the figure-background distinction—only because we are always already there "looking" for something and we do not notice or actively avoid something else. We do not have a panoramic consciousness of the world; we are in the first place a finite and partial point of view. Without this point of view, nothing at all would be given as something that is (this or that). The inauthenticity of idle talk consists in letting oneself be dominated by a generic point of view, on average shared, which certainly allows things to appear, but only in a light of obscurity and disguise because nothing "really" is what it is in such a light. The things of everyday idle talk really "are" not, even if—for this one speaks of disguise—they are also something, in a sort of suspension between Being and quasi-Being. It is not the nothing that threatens us; rather, it is confusion. (Certainly we are not denying that here there are ethical connotations, but perhaps Heidegger was right: when we think about ethics we are always referring to the conformity with a duty that is written from somewhere, therefore with a given objective.) In fact, as would appear more clearly in *Was ist Metaphysik?*, it is, if anything, the explicit relation with the nothing (experienced in anxiety) that really brings things to Being.[15] Their discovery by the authentic glance is also an instance of *Vollzugssinn*: the authentic glance does not reflect it, but brings it to true Being. It is not that things, "before," are not: the thrown project about which Heidegger speaks is something analogous, we should not forget, to Kant's a priori forms, except that here one is dealing with a radically finite and historical a priori; therefore, some given that originates "out there" corresponds to this a priori, as happened with the passivity of sensation in Kant. If anything, different from Kant (more realist) and closer to Hegel, Heidegger does not even remotely think that the "thing in itself," what would produce the stimuli on our sensible receptivity, is the true Being and that it is identified in some way with that supersensible that practical reason will postulate as the world of freedom, of God, and of the immortality of the soul. The thing in itself, to speak in these terms, is for Heidegger precisely the opaque being of the world of idle talk, just as "full" existence is that which is authentic; and thus the inauthentic, which also comes "before" (we are always already thrown), is only a "derivative" form. I will return in a bit to what are in my view the clearly religious implications of this perspective; here I only want to try to see how and why the authentic glance that brings things to true Being does not correspond to the need for descriptive objectivity, which moreover conforms to the rejection of truth as correspondence found clearly in *Being and Time*: "Sein—nicht Seiendes—'gibt es' nur, sofern Warheit ist. Und sie *ist* nur, sofern and solange Dasein ist."[16] "Being (not entities) is something which 'there is' only in so far as truth is. And truth *is* only in so far as and as long as Dasein is."[17] It is not easy to clarify the call to which Heidegger's "preference" for authenticity responds and that undoubtedly inspires his work directed at remembering the meaning of Being (beginning with the Platonic verse used as an exergue in *Being and Time*). Calling it an ethical-political demand is not arbitrary; it is an existential discomfort, and moreover similar to what was made clear in a famous page from Husserl's diary, dated September 25, 1906:

> In the first place I name the general task that I must resolve to do, if I want to call myself a philosopher. I means a *critique of reason*. A critique of logical and practical reason, of that which generally has value. I cannot truly and honestly live without clarifying the meaning, the essence, the methods, the fundamental points of view of a critique of reason. . . . I have already profited enough from the agony of the absence of clarity, from the doubt that waivers here and there. I must come to an internal solidity.[18]

Naturally, the analogy is very fragmented. Heidegger will move forward by dissolving the very idea of foundation. And to allude here to the nothing, which he expressly treats in *Was ist Metaphysik?* (even though anxiety already plays a fundamental role in *Being and Time*), is more justified than it might seem. Things come to Being as they come to the truth opened by the thrown project. This project truly makes them (come to) being only insofar as it is authentic, namely, appropriated by a Dasein who orders the world. Furthermore, it is understood: every judgment announces an order and cannot refer to an empty chaos;

an order is given only in a project and that functions as a principle of order; it becomes world only if it is individuated, if it belongs to someone. If this holds, it is an "authentic" project. But how is the project authenticated? Precisely with the assumption of the "historicity that we ourselves are" mentioned in the notes on Jaspers. This historicity is related to the nothing of *Was ist Metaphysik?* because its assumption, from *Being and Time* forward, implies the anticipatory resoluteness for death. One knows that Heidegger distinguishes this decision, obviously, from suicide and also from a sort of spiritual memento mori one finds in certain Christian religiosity. What then is he talking about? How can one articulate, certainly in "existentiell" terms (let us say, concretely understandable), the anticipatory resoluteness that "authenticates" the project? A careful investigation of the second section of *Being and Time* will, according to me, give us this conclusion. The authentic project is that which is placed in history not by taking it as *vergangen*, but as *gewesen*: not as the past, but as having-been. It is also the difference that holds between *Tradition* and *Überlieferung*: the latter term alludes to a way of placing oneself in relation with the past by taking it as open possibility, as the call to an active-interpretative continuation, provider of a *Vollzugssinn*; *Tradition* mummifies the past, or worse, considers it the object of a "scientific" historiography, which reaches its goal when it believes to have described it exhaustively (precisely, by exhausting its meaning). Why does an authentic understanding of historicity have anything to do with the anticipatory resoluteness for death? As with death, the permanent possibility of the impossibility of every possibility, it makes the concrete possibilities possible by positioning them in their state of being possible, by allowing "discussion" among them, which turns them into a historically living con-text; thus for Dasein, knowing oneself to be mortal means knowing that the others from whom one is born are also mortal, taking on their inheritance as a possibility that is offered and not, like nature or necessity, as the objectivity of which one takes note.[19] One sees here, among other things, how much the problematic of the human sciences, or of Weberian *Wertfreiheit* (which

Heidegger discusses explicitly in the notes on Jaspers, pages 34–36), comes in to construct the core of Heideggerian philosophy, which for this reason is also legitimately called hermeneutic ontology.

Things and the world are discovered in their true Being only in light of a mortal project, which inherits its opening from other mortal projects. True Being is marked by this partiality—of the point of view, of the finite and positioned project, and of the temporality that continually denies any (metaphysical) claims of permanence and eternity. The difficulty of speaking about the anticipatory resoluteness for death in existentiell and concrete terms derives from the fact that one does not "take note" of one's own death, or even of simple mortality, as if it were an objective given—one can only live it. The relation to death, ultimately, is the archetype of the *Vollzugssinn*, primarily for the banal reason that, psychologically, a possible and detached contemplation of this given is never presented to us, even before the fact that one cannot be a spectator of one's own death.

But is this still ontology, or only anthropology, or psychology? Could we think that all of this being marked by mortality concerns only Dasein and not Being itself? Yes, but only if we were to attribute in a preliminary manner the quality of the object "out there" to Being itself by supposing that reality in itself, the true and meaningful reality, is that which appears in the neutrality of idle talk, or even in the scientific-objective discourse that is, in an uncritical way, identified with the true discourse. Once we are placed before the choice in Parmenides's poem, between the path of day and the path of night, the options can no longer be avoided; even if we choose the path of error, *we choose* it, and so idle talk is also a project, but a closed and opaque project. This project, outside of every moralistic assessment, is given as the derivation that is less full than the other and authentic one that belongs to someone.

It was already noted, I believe, that the title of *Being and Time* actually means Being *is* Time. But this "*is*" cannot be read as the *ist* of objective description; it is supremely *vollzugssinnig*, or *vollzugssinnlich*, we could risk saying. It is a proposition that we can state only as we are doing it, while we live our Being and mortal being in a world of things that are given to us in personal projects that we ourselves are.

The "reality" of the world that discloses itself in the authentic project of Dasein is more "true" than what is captured in the daily media and in the inauthenticity of idle talk. It has the force and the concreteness, for example, of Newton's laws, which Heidegger discusses in section 44c of *Being and Time*.[20] The scientific project, thematically pursued and not confused with the *naturaliter* realistic glance that ought to be the basis of every other experience, gives rise to a type of "true Being" that hermeneutic ontology not only refuses to demonize, but, in fact, authentically legitimates.

These results of a directed, but not arbitrary, reading of (a part of) *Being and Time* can be developed in many directions. What matters for our discussion is to see how from the involvement of the interpreter in the event, in the game of interpretation—that in Nietzsche was announced but then was forgotten by him and by many who have moved close to him in the hermeneutic *koiné*—one reaches a solution to the problem that we have called the "hurdy-gurdy song." The world and things come to true Being, in the light of an interpretation that is not the same as any other, insofar as the project that makes them come into discovery is positioned explicitly in an event of mortality. The Kantian a priori has become, in Heidegger, the inheritance of mortals and other mortals; what we inherit from it, we can now say, is not the idea (eternal, stable) of Being, but the history of Being. To return to McDowell (discussed in the previous chapter), one can pass from the extreme punctuality of private experience, which would not give rise to any proposition justified and valid for everyone, to the truth only by inserting the brute given into the network of the "thinkable,"[21] namely, if we follow Heidegger, the concrete historical opening into which we are thrown. There is something like a history of Being precisely because Being is not eternal, is not modeled on the opaque stability of the inauthentic way that things are given in their everyday banality. Historical ages are given only insofar as Being itself is characterized by epochality, by its suspension. Will it be the sort of suspension characterizable as the retreat of God spoken of in negative theology? If we think of it in this way, it would still be from the perspective of metaphysical ontology and "existentialistic" anthropology: for whatever Being there is, it is full and eternal, but nonetheless inaccessible to us. It is possible that Heidegger has been at times (mis)understood in these terms, according to a line that we can say comes from the "Heideggerian right."[22] It rather seems to me more faithful to the spirit, if not always to the letter, of his thought to read the relation between being, true being, and being-unto-death as a vocation of Being that is given only as the negation of any (claimed) reality "out there." The languages that constitute the (epochal or specialized) horizons in which truth is given are not multiple ways or efforts to descriptively measure the real out there: they are ways in which that "real" becomes true, by coming to Being— that it is intimately oriented toward being given as the suspension of the peremptoriness of presence and immediacy, within horizons that are "lived" and therefore also "mortal." All of this in Heidegger comes from the originary existential refusal of the idea of Being as the sheer presence of beings. Refused, we do not forget it, motivated by the experience of freedom, which would be incomprehensible and denied in a world made essentially of "objectivity" and "givenness." The affirmation of freedom, we could say, has a price: that of mortality, which not only touches the Being of humanity, but characterizes Being itself—to take note of freedom and make it possible, Being cannot be thought as givenness, eternal structure, pure Aristotelian act, or Parmenidean Being. It is legitimate to speak of a nihilistic vocation of Being for all of this, as if its history were intimately moved by a paradoxical teleology asymptotically directed toward a nothing that, obviously, will never be able to be realized as a metaphysical state, as the actual reality of the nothing. We are also speaking of nihilism here because the being given of Being only as suspension, the negation of the peremptoriness of beings, is in its turn the result of a history that Nietzsche was the first to recognize,[23] and to which Heidegger also corresponds with his critique of metaphysics. Is the history of Being the history of metaphysics, in which "nothing remains of Being as such" in the history of the West, of the *Abendland*, of the setting of Being?[24] Only our history? But we could say this about it only if we repositioned ourselves in the metaphysical perspective that thinks Being as a given "out there," namely, in that objectivism (authoritarian, inauthentic) that Heidegger struggles to overcome.

THE AGE OF THE WORLD PICTURE

T he world picture that determines our age, and that gave the title to Heidegger's essay from 1938 contained in *Holzwege*,[1] is the picture of the world that is given by experimental science and by the positive sciences in general. At the start of the essay, in fact, Heidegger characterizes the modern age as dominated and de-fined by science—whose model is, in many senses, experimental science (already in Dilthey the human sciences "must" be given a method, different than but analogous to—for rigor and in other ways—that of the natural sciences). How can we read this expression, the age of the world picture, in light of the conclusions from the previous chapter? Remember that there it was a matter of the interpretative character of every experience of the world, and of the importance of truth in this experience, which appeared to us tied to the authenticity of the project; authenticity, in its turn, is achievable only by virtue of the anticipatory resoluteness for death, that is, according to our interpretation, by the force of the explicit assumption of the historicity of existing, which is such only within the framework of the history of Being.

As I already said, this is not only, or principally, to illustrate Heidegger's thought historiographically, with the pretense of presenting it in a faithful manner; rather, we are trying to develop a discussion of reality that accounts for the contribution—a defining one for us—of this thinker; but its defining feature is the sort that occurs within the frame of an interpretation that is not at all obvious, that does not claim to have value as the pure illustration of that thought. Thus, if we now turn to the question of science—let us define it thus, generically, for now—it is not only because this movement is required by the very development of Heideggerian thought, beginning with the pages in *Being and Time* where, in the final pages of the first section (where there is truth only insofar as Dasein is), he speaks of the "reality" of Newton's laws.

More generally, it is a matter of fact that the historical-social weight and importance of the experimental sciences in our time do not seem to allow themselves to be read in light of a hermeneutics that not only wants to correspond with the inheritance of Nietzsche (there are no facts, only interpretations) but also wants to follow it through to its extreme consequences (on the tracks of the nihilistic Heidegger, thinker of the history of Being). In effect, however paradoxical it might seem, the contemporary picture of science, implicitly shared by many sciences, widespread among epistemologists, and considered at least admissible whether by them or by the mass public,[2] is more easily described in Nietzschean terms (every scientific proposition is proved only within its paradigms, in the Kuhnian sense of the term, but the coming about of the paradigms is completely by chance, is unpredictable, and has at best a logic of the evolutionary sort described by Darwin, which is not guided by any rule: ultimately, it is event) rather than in Heideggerian terms. How can we in fact apply the more radical aspects of hermeneutics to the work of science, starting from the connection between the authentic opening of the entity in its Being and its authentic project—decided in an anticipatory way for one's own death? It would seem that the only way to avoid scandalizing the scientists and the common mindset too much would be by reserving the radical experience of "authentic" truth for philosophy or in general for thought in its most pregnant and existential sense, the sense for which, according to another scandalous claim by Heidegger that is often repeated as an accusation in his debates, "science does not think." This division of tasks, which perhaps in the end will show it has at least some sense, but only after many clarifications (it is true that it will touch on thought and "philosophy" in some way to authenticate the sciences, according to a schema that one finds in *Was ist Metaphysik?*), if taken literally, is too simplistic: it accounts neither for the history of terms such as "metaphysics," "ontology," "philosophy," and "science" in the long course of Heidegger's thinking, nor first of all for the fact that at least for an early part of this itinerary Heidegger speaks explicitly of philosophy as he would a science, even as the supreme science.[3] Nonetheless, above all we want to understand if and by what measure what we have concluded by reading and interpreting *Being and Time* matters for the work of science—namely, that only to an authentically open Dasein is an entity given in what it properly, really, authentically is. The world cannot appear before a neutral and unbiased glance, just as a book speaks only to the one who looks for something there (maybe even only by remaining deluded, denied, and so on); and it appears much more in its very own truth the more that the glance is clearly oriented. Staying with the example of a book, it speaks to us much more when our expectations are qualified, we could say "intended." This is not the case of a book or a spectacle to which we are drawn only because "it has something to say." The anonymous "they," as *Being and Time* says, is on the contrary also a project, but due to its anonymity it only allows a disguised image of things to appear. It is useless, or perhaps not, to remember that here we are nonetheless in the framework of an idea of truth that is not measured according to the "objectivity" of things as simply present. It is not as objects held within a totality of their aspects that things are given to authentically open Dasein in their own authentic truth, or instead flee to the anonymous project of the "they." Here it seems there is, or there really is, a circle; or better, it is already a consequence of the existential analytic and of its notion of world as a system of equipment, always and only articulated within a project. Any "neutrality" is therefore inauthentic, especially in the sense—for which one could evoke Marx, the critic of ideology—that it hides its very projectural character, by claiming (even with the authoritarian implications brought to light by Nietzsche's work "On Truth and Lying in a Non-Moral Sense") to have value as the pure objective truth, a notion that, before ever disguising individual things, is revealed as untenable (even the antiskeptical argument, applied here, is presented as a pure act of force: mine is not an interpretation, it is the truth; or even, it is only the final truth that we ought to seek, not an interpretation valid here for both of us).

Furthermore, that the problem of science asserts itself precisely as that with which all accounts must be settled, first of all from the point of view of a nihilistic hermeneutic ontology, is an example of the "impurity" of our (and Heidegger's) moving forward. I already stated that the Heideggerian return to the problem of the meaning of Being does not seem to me to be motivated by purely "theoretical" reasons (if it is admitted that the expression might have a meaning); the reduction of Being to objectness, which gives rise to the rule of the world's total organization (what Heidegger really, basically, escapes, in perfect consonance with the spirit of the avant-garde), is first of all the work of the final transformation of metaphysics (Platonic and the like) into experimental science, where only what is in fact verified in a mathematically directed and planned experiment truly *is*. The debate about the natural sciences and the human sciences at the beginning of the twentieth century, and the same phenomenological undertaking by Husserl (which seems more tied, in its inspiration, to the dispute over the foundations of mathematics), to which Heidegger, as a scholar of philosophy, is profoundly tied, can also be read as a "conflict of the Faculties" in the academic sense of the term, as an impatience for the rule of the positive scientists not only within the bounds of the university, but in the social world in general.

Nonetheless, it is not a coincidence that I dwelled for so long on these topics. What is important to understand is that, if we say that there are no facts but only interpretations, and above all if, by going beyond Nietzsche with (our) Heidegger, we say that this too is an interpretation and that it demands to be developed in the nihilistic sense of the history of Being, we ought to reckon with the "realistic" claims of experimental science. On the other hand, it is true that much of epistemology today, far more than at the beginning of the twentieth century, is willing to admit the interpretative character of scientific knowledge. But, at least it seems to us, it does so without ever going beyond a generic form of perspectivism, which remains deeply metaphysical to the degree that it believes to be able to speak of the plurality of interpretations from a point of view that is naively panoramic and never really involved in the process. What changes, for the conception of science and above all for that of the reality which interests us here, if we adopt a nihilistic ontology that to us seems implicit in the Heideggerian idea of the history of Being? One "arrives" at the history of Being by beginning with the question of the possible nonequivalence of all interpretations: thus, precisely by posing a problem that is at once epistemological and metaepistemological. In a strictly epistemological sense, the perspectivism of the hermeneutic *koiné* is able to admit that a proposition is verified (or falsified, in a Popperian way) only within the paradigms that in their turn are never completely verifiable. I remember a fierce debate with John Searle (where I had David Farrell Krell as my ally), whose thesis was as follows: let us agree that our paradigms are historically conditioned, we know that; now *let's get to work*, let's begin to utilize them by applying ourselves to real research. We are always within an opening (historical, destinal, unforeseeable) of truth. We can do nothing but act within it, otherwise the discussion ends up having no rules and no criterion—by definition, there is no ulterior paradigm by which one could judge the truth or falsehood of the opening (of the paradigm) within which we currently stand. One will remember that in the preface to *Was ist Metaphysik?* from 1929, Heidegger was ultimately posing such a question: the sciences are concerned with their object and "nothing" else—in this way, however, they encounter the problem of the nothing.

What Heidegger calls metaphysics (still without the polemic sense that he would attribute to it in later writings), the "science" that poses the question about the nothing and that science "rejects" by focusing on its task of positive and rigorous investigation, is the terrain of philosophy, of ontology, or, when all of these terms are abandoned, of thought. In this sense, and only this, Heidegger claims that "science does not think."[4] To repeat without following, the transformations that this set of terms suffers in the development of Heideggerian thought, let us say here that thought (metaphysics, ontology, philosophy) is distinguished from the sciences because it is not bound to assume its (own) opening of truth as the ultimate given, but rather poses the question about the truth of that opening. If, as it seems (as cultural anthropology teaches, the historical-political experience of the end of Eurocentrism and, before that, the existential analytic that refused to give to the project that we ourselves are the stability of the objects that appear within it), the opening into which we are thrown is historical, mutable, and finite, then thought will be able to and must be able to pose the question of its truth. It does so in a new way, but not in an objectivistic and descriptive sense—how it ultimately remains in the case of the various schools of suspicion, especially in the Marxist critique of ideology. But in what sense then? Here one returns to the final thesis in the first section of *Being and Time*: "Being (not entities) is something which 'there is' only in so far as truth *is*. And truth *is* only in so far as and as long as Dasein is."[5] A coherent nihilistic and ontological reading of this thesis cannot but emphasize the difference between Being and entities by shedding light on the significance of a real juxtaposition. What is at stake when one speaks of Being and of truth is not the presence of the immediate given (of "reality," if one wants). Furthermore, let us remember, in a completely different perspective, the reading of the Kantian a priori proposed by McDowell: it is not the simple presence of a given to a subject that grounds truth, but the interpretative insertion (let us add) of this immediate given into the network of concepts, a network that McDowell also identified with a second, and that means historical and inherited, nature.

Therefore, the first conclusion: the truth of the opening under investigation here cannot be conceived in terms of the faithful representation of the thing that appears in that opening. We can only search for such a truth on the level of the project's authenticity. In the authentic project, assumed by someone as one's own, the thing can appear as what it really is because it escapes from the opacity covering it in the anonymous project of the "they." The example that seemed clearest is found in the deep personal interest one takes in a book, which "really" says something only in this light, while it tends to escape us when we want it only in virtue of the anonymous project of the "they." Will the book appear to have a more "objective" truth when we have an authentic interest (project) in it? Immediately one sees that this hypothesis does not make sense. The "objective" reality of the book could in fact be that of its actual existence on the shelves of the bookstore, in the warehouse of the publisher, in the critical discussion that reviewers give of it, or the sum of all of these aspects (but managed by whom, and why, and therefore with which pretense of completion?). All of this tells us that we can speak of truth, acquired at one time in the results of the existential analytic, only in terms of "sense," of the sense that a given has (acquires from the beginning) within a project. A sense that is all the more true the more the project is "appropriated" (by someone, and for that reason also "in terms of the thing"). (The Sartre of *Being and Nothingness* had certainly read *Being and Time*; this makes sense, up to a certain point, due to the fact that sense, the "for me" of the thing, removes the "in itself," or therefore opposes it. But Sartre is still always guided by an ontic conception of Being, as that which is given, solid, and so on. Sense does not have "reality" and thus is the nothing.) The truth of sense, the Being of beings, certainly does not claim to take the place of its everyday entity—as in Heidegger, authentic existence remains difficult to describe in existentiell, concrete terms. Nevertheless, to act in the realm of sense and not the realm of the ontic presence of the thing does not simply mean leaving things as they are. The relations between the two levels are by now more complicated than they were, and this is exactly the case as it is in play in the Heideggerian and nihilistic overcoming of the perspectivism of the hermeneutic *koiné*.

Even from this point of view, Dasein's entire relation with the world is to be reconsidered according to the sentence we have already cited: Being, and not entities. The being given of the thing in average everydayness, which already involves its placement in a project, in an opening, is also a way of overcoming the pure "entity" and moving toward Being, of overcoming, to a further degree, scientific thematization. Here because, most likely, even science cannot undertake its practice without a reference to being-unto-death.

Let us consider it again: to stand calmly within the opening of truth assigned to us (Searle's *let's get to work*) is not possible, except through a deliberate choice that nonetheless ought to be justified as a project and therefore ought to offer some argument regarding its own preferability—what is the "truth of the opening." The question regarding this latter option is not avoided except with the final "and nothing else" of the scientific will (this is the job; we go to work; I pay for this; my task is that), namely, with an authoritarian gesture (which is such even when one submits to it without challenging an authority: exactly what is prescribed by the division of social labor) that moreover corresponds to the deeply authoritarian character of metaphysics (one no longer asks questions when confronted by the ultimate foundation). The Heideggerian notion of authenticity, with all of its unanswered problems, is not at all very far from the most everyday experience: to question the meaning of one's own job, to ask why one takes on certain tasks and duties, happens to everyone, and in the end the "answer," the sort that is never complete, encounters the question of mortality in the various ways that it appears in one's self-interrogation (the hope in a beyond, the awareness of the nondeterministic nature of the various possibilities actually given to us in existence, the accepted or rejected bond with an inheritance—the home, fatherland, or the church, about which Stephen Dedalus speaks).[6] I am only accenting a way of "urbanizing," of making understandable, the Heideggerian connection between the authenticity of the project and the anticipatory resoluteness for death, a connection that seems particularly problematic when one speaks of scientific knowledge.

One could also show that the authenticity that is established—if it is being established, or appears as possible—in the decision for death resolves Weber's problems of formal and material rationality: as long as you are not sure of yourself, undertake the work of the scientist in an inauthentic way; but does that mean with less efficacy? It is the same question asked in Husserl's *Krisis*: the sciences function even without the transcendental foundation of phenomenology. The initial Heideggerian solution, let's say from *Being and Time* to *What Is Metaphysics?*, is one that is fundamentally conciliatory: scientists might also work, but philosophy speaks of the transcendental and for this reason is still called a science, and indeed the most fundamental one. And what else? The more the argument about the history of Being becomes clear in Heidegger, the less the division of labor between the philosopher and scientist holds up.

With the preface to *What Is Metaphysics?*, published in 1929, nonetheless written in the shadow of the publication of *Being and Time*, Heidegger provided two important indications for clarifying the connection between the project and the anticipatory resoluteness for death: on the one side, it presents metaphysics as a science, or in any case as a form of knowledge, a discipline that in some way stands at the base of all the others (it seems to me this point is clarified, albeit not in an exhaustive way, in the postscript to *What Is Metaphysics?*, written in 1943); on the other side—this is already rather clear in the text from 1929—there is the idea that "scientific existence is possible only if in advance it holds itself out into the nothing."[7] In the postscript, metaphysics is already, more explicitly than in the preface of 1929, the thinking that "remains concerned with beings and does not turn itself to Being as Being." Even in this way, nevertheless, it is a thinking that "in its answers to the question concerning beings as such . . . operates with a prior representation of Being." That does not contradict what Heidegger writes in the preface from 1929: "metaphysics is inquiry beyond or over beings that aims to recover them as such and as a whole for our grasp." Therefore, and even with noticeable but not influential terminological differences regarding our question here, the two texts say the same thing: metaphysics stands alongside the particular sciences in the manner described by the citation from Descartes that begins the preface: metaphysics is the root from which all of the other sciences begin. This is so because the metaphysical question per excellence is the one formulated in the famous question from Leibniz: why, in general, is there something rather than nothing? Not only does metaphysics not respond to this question, but it even formulates it poorly, because its thinking proceeds with the "constantly lurking possibility of deepest error," an error that will become clear in the postscript (it only treats the totality of beings). And so, the particular sciences hide by not considering the nothing (they are concerned with something and nothing else); metaphysics has the merit of questioning beyond beings, toward the nothing; but even metaphysics "returns" only to the totality of beings, and for that reason needs an overcoming, as is understood in the postscript. Even without yet speaking of overcoming, the preface from 1929 indicates in what direction thinking must move if it is to take the question of the nothing seriously and thus "really" to function as the "foundation" of the sciences that, as noted in the citation from Descartes in the postscript, it assumes as its task. In the preface, Heidegger speaks to the academic community: "Our existence—in the community of researchers, teachers, and students—is determined by science"; what is articulated in the various sciences, whether they are the natural sciences or the human sciences, is that they each have their own specific rigor, and that they have a "relation to the world" in common, namely, the fact of excluding, on principle, the question of the nothing. In science—as the effort of inquiring, determining, grounding—"a submission to beings themselves" is realized: "In this pursuit nothing less transpires than the irruption by one being called 'the human being' into the whole of beings, indeed in such a way that in and through this irruption beings break open and show what they are and how they are." *Being and Time* also speaks (see especially section 32) of letting beings appear in what really is; and the lecture course on Kant from 1927–28 speaks of the scientific attitude as the will to bring beings out into the open "*um seines Enthülltseins willen*" (in view of its being discovered).[8] Dasein, in *Being and Time*, is discovering. In short, to let being appear as such remains the task of science, even if Heidegger theorizes the hermeneutic character of the experience of truth. And this letting appear, in *What Is Metaphysics?*, and already in *Being and Time*, is possible in virtue of (the manifesting of, or the leaving aside of) the nothing. For the preface of 1929, where the history of Being is not yet thematized, the connection consists in the fact that "only because the nothing is manifest in the ground of Dasein can the total strangeness overwhelm us. Only when the strangeness of beings oppresses us does it arouse and evoke wonder."[9] To me this does not seem to be a sufficient connection, even if it comes to an end with what Heidegger says in the first pages of the preface, where he speaks of the sense of doing science for scientists, a sense that is not separable from the argument in *Being and Time* about the authenticity of existence, but in this case is not explicitly set forth.

As I have said many times, we find in these Heideggerian texts some suggestions and some indications that without any sense of superiority appear to complete and make explicit even terms that one does not encounter in Heidegger. The problematic light in which the connection between science and the nothing appears in *What Is Metaphysics?* is easily explained: it deals with a connection of a purely psychological and anthropological type (not coincidentally tied to a moment when Heidegger no longer speaks of the history of Being) in which the existentials (the "structures" of existence discovered by the analytic of *Being and Time*) still seem constants, projectedness always already thrown, but exactly, "always, already," in a historicity that coincides with the finitude of *Befindlichkeit*, of the affective situation, and nothing more. The opening toward the nothing found in the preface from 1929, through the analysis of the experience of anxiety, is still only a beginning— as can be expected, after all, given the "occasional" character of the text. We understand its significance only if we place that opening in relation to the nihilistic reading of the conclusion of the first section of *Being and Time*: "There is Being and not entities." The experience of truth is inseparably tied to the experience of the nothing: anxiety is more clearly tied to Being unto death; and the anticipatory resoluteness for death is the assumption of one's own constitutive historicity, thus the immersion in the nothing as the nihilistic history of Being (and not—only—of entities).

But once again, if we do not want to stick to the simple yet somewhat banal argument about wonder in *What Is Metaphysics?*, what does the immersion in the nothing *and thus* in the history of Being mean for science? Does one manage to understand in what sense a scientist who has authentically decided for his own death would succeed in letting entities appear in their truth better than someone who remains calmly within the average everydayness of the "they"? One should keep in mind that this question is in this way only marginally within a Heideggerianism that in the end can be rediscovered, in merely analogous terms, but certainly, in the Husserl of the *Krisis*. There, the crisis of the sciences does not really mean that they might "function" less effectively from the point of view of the validity of their results and the efficacy of their technical applications. However, lacking the ultimate and explicit foundation that Husserl seeks, they do not correspond to the vocation—albeit historical, not natural, but by now it has become unavoidable, for the same reasons that one no longer goes to the witchdoctor after the birth of scientific medicine—that modern science inherited from its Greek origins. In the case of Heidegger, the point—which is clarified progressively over the course of years, but that is already clearly present in *Being and Time*—is that letting the thing appear in its truth does not in fact mean it is described objectively, completely, and exhaustively. It means that it is inserted explicitly into a project that one knows and wants. For example, in the project of seeking entities for the love of their being sought. Science, with its "distinctive relation to the world in which we turn toward beings themselves" that seeks to "approach what is essential in all things," is "a freely chosen stance of human existence."[10] By now it ought to be clear to us: in

Heidegger there is no logos intended as discourse that is fundamentally representative of things as they "are." Such a discourse is always only a derivative of the truth of the Being of beings. The scientist who lives an authentic existence—admitting that this might ever be possible— is better at letting the truth of the entities he studies appear because, even when they are placed into an "objectifying" perspective, however neutral, which derives from subjective interests, he knows that this is a deliberate choice of human existence, one possible relation to the world among many others.[11] The anxiety discussed in the preface is still too psychological, too "existentialistic" to satisfy any further development of the discourse that belongs to us and, let us also believe, to Heidegger. If the scientific project must be assumed as a deliberate choice of human existence, it cannot be motivated by that hurdy-gurdy song by which there are many ways of approaching the world, lest I find myself performing the work of the scientist, *let's go to work*, allowing that it is done in the best way that I know. Moreover, "there are" not many ways, statistically given, of approaching the world. The plurality of linguistic games and the specialization of the sciences are not a static articulation, are not categories, one can say with *Being and Time*, even in the sense that there are not Kantian transcendentals as eternal aspects of reason. There are existentials, namely, ways of being for Dasein in its historicity.

Being and Time opened the path for placing the various linguistic games into the history of Being. This is accomplished through the idea that the project is "authenticated" only in the anticipatory resoluteness for death, and *that is*, according to me, in the explicit engagement of one's own radical historicity. The more it becomes clear to Heidegger that this engagement with historicity means placing the existentials into the history of Being—the inauthenticity of *Being and Time* becomes metaphysics as the forgetting of Being in the later works, and Eigen-*tlichkeit* (authenticity) gives up its place, even terminologically, to *Ere*ignis (event)[12]—the less the relation between thinking (no longer called metaphysics, or ontology, or even philosophy) and the sciences is maintained within a stable framework. "There is Being (not entities)" could still seem like the foundation for a division of tasks: the sciences speak about entities, and the relation to Being (and to the nothing) is secured by philosophy, which stands at the root of every other form of knowledge as described by Descartes's tree and, earlier, by Porphyry and all of the Western tradition. But Being also has a history, and its epochality makes the ages of the world possible; the thrownness of Dasein and the multiple languages in which it is articulated are historically changeable. Beginning with the essay on the work of art from 1936, Heidegger no longer speaks of being *in the* world, but of being *in a* world. To choose the project of scientific objectivity or another project, within that general project—always given it seems inauthentically, which is that of the belonging to an age—implies that Dasein "chooses its heroes," namely, that Dasein thematizes its own provenance, takes it not as an obvious necessity, but as a still always open possibility. The truth (existential, certainly, not objective-descriptive, which in any case is an illusion)[13] of science requires that one even chooses the project of submitting to entities—and this is always understood better since science became a grand social enterprise, with the investment of ends, various forms of conditioning, political or not, and so on. Certainly, the immediate "given," the encounter-discovery with an event that falsifies or verifies a proposition, remains; but we are now dealing with an event that makes sense only within the outline of a hypothesis—also in the sense of a pure and simple Popperian falsification that does not immediately interfere with being-unto-death, but that still has strong links with a general projectuality; if it remains implicit, no one doubts that leaving it in such an opaque state involves less freedom in the exercise of science. What serves or doesn't a more effective completion of the scientist's job, the call of the philosopher to the anticipatory resoluteness for death, that is, to the explicit recognition and engagement of one's own historicity, is a call to increased freedom. ("Without the originary manifestness of the nothing, no selfhood and no freedom,"[14] because without the conscious engagement of historicity science itself tends to fashion itself as the passive contemplation of an order of fixed objects, or at least as the fulfillment of tasks [the social order] accepted as obvious and indisputable.)

The call to freedom is not a way to leap outside of problems by evoking a value that "wins" because it is undeniable. On the one side, it conforms to the avant-garde inspiration that to us seemed to have been known at the origin of thought in Heidegger; on the other side, freedom is here synonymous with "sense," that is, with selfhood, not so much arbitrary freedom, as it is an existence that unfolds in a discursivity granted with a direction and a lived continuity.

Will placing oneself in the history of Being, by choosing one's own heroes and thus by hazarding an interpretation of one's own constitutive origin, also mean setting aside the reference to the nothing that the introduction from 1929 thematized in somewhat anxiously psychologistic terms? What remains of the existentialist Heidegger from the earlier works in this Heidegger, thinker of the history of Being? In this regard, even the reflection on science gives meaningful indications. The history of Being is the history of its happening in the configurations that give order to its various ages, we could say, of the *archai* that are in force in any age and that constitute its opening.[15] For our modern age, science intended as an experimental enterprise that is rigorously organized and subdivided into various realms, tasks, and so on is its "defining" element.[16] But this is not a static characterization: our age becomes, brings metaphysics to its end, above all because science has developed in a certain way.

The relatively pacifying separation of metaphysics and science that one reads in *What Is Metaphysics?* is also overwhelmed by the idea, the historicity of Being, that becomes central in Heidegger at least by 1936. In the lecture "The Age of the World Picture" from 1938, experimental science separated from metaphysics becomes a defining agent in the dissolution of metaphysics. The systematic construction of the world picture that characterizes modern science "founded" upon metaphysics ends up being articulated in so many subdivisions that their totality becomes unmanageable. But this very systematicity, that which Nietzsche in

"On Truth and Lying in a Non-Moral Sense" called the immense *columbarium* of concepts, is what culminates as an explosion at the peak of modernity. Also or perhaps only because of this explosion, which renders the world picture impossible, so too metaphysics—whether in the sense of special science that still operates in *What Is Metaphysics?*, or as the forgetting of Being (and thus of the nothing) that favors the prevailing view of universalized objectivity and reduces Being to the level of the totality of entities, of objects—becomes impossible; those same entities are lost in the Babel of languages and specialized areas in which no one can claim to be master or holder of a "world picture." The very idea of a history of Being becomes unthinkable, in the sense that it can no longer be conceived as a history; here one can also see one of the reasons for the growing preference in Heidegger for the term and the idea of the event. If one can speak of a continuity, it presents itself only within the outline of a project, of an interpretation—"Dasein chooses its heroes." The project is also—although usually only at the level of the "they," of the fore-understanding of a society, of an age, of a community—the project of experimental science. The "openings of truth," that is, the ages of Being (the ways in which it lets entities appear by being suspended, concealed), are like the historical-natural language that every Dasein finds itself speaking, the culture into which one is thrown. There is no "natural" being-thrown from which the "authentic" project belonging to an existing being might have to free itself. The "natural" condition into which we are thrown, and against whose background one can find authentic engagement, is nothing but the crystallization of prior existential decisions; ultimately, this is all that we call "reality." This is something analogous to what happens in the relation between *langue* and *parole* in the linguistics of Saussure: every *parole*, every actual use of the language on the part of the speaker, leaves a trace that modifies, or can modify, the *langue*—vocabulary, syntax, and so on. But the inheritance of these variations lives only in the reading that is made by another speaker—that is, in another event. It does not have the "reality" of an "objectively" given process.

INTERMISSION

THE TEMPTATION OF REALISM

I speak about the "temptation" of realism because, as with true temptations, it is something that returns and torments us. By wanting to be "realists" for real, so to speak, one must come to terms with the reality of this permanent temptation.

Let's begin with the famous maxim from Nietzsche, according to which "there are no facts, only interpretations." It must be remembered that in the context in which he is writing (a notebook from 1886–87) Nietzsche also added, "and this too is an interpretation [*Auslegung*]." Is it so obvious that, especially with this phrase, Nietzsche's maxim is equal to a metaphysical affirmation of the unreality of the world, to a type of empirical idealism à la Berkeley? For example, some attribute this sort of idealism even to Richard Rorty, who speaks explicitly of philosophies (and works of art, and individual Weltanschauungen, and even scientific paradigms) as "redescriptions" of the world—therefore supposing that, nevertheless, something like a world, the world, might be given, even if accessible only and always from a point of view opened by a redescription. In the case of Nietzsche, neither is the reality of the world reduced to the perception of the subject, nor does the perceiving subject have an ontological directive more solid than his claimed "illusions." What matters here in Nietzsche, as in Rorty and in contemporary hermeneutic ontology, is not a metaphysical option that favors irrealism (idealism) over realism. The "game of interpretations" is not at all a collection of arbitrary movements in which the subject, consciously, or even by abandoning itself surrealistically to its own creative unconscious, creates a picture of "reality" to compare to the reality of others. The game is in fact always also a conflict; to use a term that is less harsh probably only means indicating a telos, a regulative ideal toward which to move; that is exactly what happens to the Nietzschean notion of will to power, which not only and definitively refers to a clash of physical forces for the purpose of overpowering others, but precisely in its movement of going beyond also overtakes the various concretizations of power, the "interests" of individual centers of will (about whose "reality" and finality Nietzsche justly harbors many doubts).

Therefore, to think the game of interpretations first of all as conflict, or the redescriptions as something that is measured with descriptions already given, or the Kuhnian paradigms as openings that resemble the not always tranquil institution of new tables of values, or the Heideggerian event of truth exactly as event, as gap and discontinuity, and also as uncanniness and anxiety—would all of this really be referable to an illusionistic ontology, to the aestheticism of a conception of reality that is totally "virtual," that ought no longer to reckon with the concrete weight of the technical means that make it possible?

In opposition to hermeneutics, and to the ontology that it presupposes (more or less explicitly and consciously), the realists are guilty exactly of too little realism: they do not manage to grasp and describe "adequately" the experience from which it arises, on which, if one prefers, it is grounded. And yet, this experience is what in fact constitutes the "reality" of many contemporary philosophies: from Nietzsche to Heidegger to the entire galaxy of postmodern thought, but also the various schools of psychoanalysis and of many postanalytic philosophical and epistemological positions. Can the Nietzschean problematic of the death of God and the Heideggerian one of the overcoming of metaphysics (which can be reunited under the shared category of nihilism, and which give rise to what a rigorously metaphysical logic defines as a performative contradiction) be removed from the panorama of contemporary thought only by recalling the principle of noncontradiction? Has the logical argument against skepticism ever convinced anyone to abandon his skeptical "convictions"?

It seems that this very realism, faced with a phenomenon as complex and vast as that of the widespread nihilism in today's culture and existence (the hermeneutic *koiné* in its various aspects), ought to refuse to explain it as the result of a common logical error, as if an entire culture were to unexpectedly forget the principle of noncontradiction. I am underlining this paradox because it seems essential. While Heidegger, and not only he, beginning from the turn in the 1930s, was forced to "justify" his own philosophy in epochal terms—which I would also call empirical terms, in the sense of experience as a fact not reducible to the impression on the tabula rasa of the mind—the realists, in this case, by referring to a logical oversight, try to sort out from the beginning the world about which hermeneutics wants to be the theory and interpretation. Moreover, it is a reference that has always considered itself to be the victorious argument but has never functioned as such. I had proposed to speak about the culture—not only philosophical—of the late industrial, postmodern, Western world, of a hermeneutic *koiné* that belongs to us. As with all fore-understandings, even this one is a vague picture, which seems to be marked too much by a sort of philosophical-sociological impressionism; to many it appears, not without reason, as a far too ambitious generalization that unifies a multiplicity of completely heterogeneous phenomena. Nevertheless, taking on the risk of bringing our attention to the hermeneutic *koiné* as a comprehensive, and vague, characteristic of our present culture is indispensible for any deep theoretical understanding of it that is able to grasp an interpretative guiding thread. This is the first step toward an "ontology of the present" [*ontologia dell'attualità*], that is, toward a thinking that goes beyond the metaphysical forgetting of Being, a forgetting that is perpetuated to the point that thinking is maintained in a confused fragmentation of specialized forms of knowledge and multiple social roles into which we moderns find ourselves thrown.

Hermeneutics, as we know, is the philosophy whose focal point is the phenomenon of interpretation, namely, a consciousness of the real that does not think of itself as the objective reflection of the things "out there," but as a stance that carries in itself the mark of someone who "knows." Luigi Pareyson defines it as "consciousness of forms by persons," a *nachschaffen* in which the knowing subject grasps the thing insofar as that subject, by reconstructing the thing as form, also expresses itself in this reconstruction because it develops and exploits a basic similarity that can have differing degrees but that is never absent from the whole. Does it make sense to conceive of consciousness in these terms? To begin with, one can reasonably think that the similarity that Pareyson discusses (that he, let us remember, recognizes as the basis for the consciousness of others and of aesthetic experience) is not very far from that which Kant called the schematism. Whatever might be the value of this combination, we should remember that the hermeneutics of today is a continuation of Kantianism, albeit remote. The world is phenomenon, that is, an order of things that the subject enters into and constructs actively. In Kant, however, there is still the idea that the a priori structures of the subject might be equal in all rational, finite beings. In the twentieth century, after Heidegger, these structures come to be recognized in their radical historicity. Not only do we never know anything other than phenomena, but they are given only in the framework of what Heidegger calls a "thrown project." To know, already at the level of the pure and simple spatiotemporal perceptions, means constructing a background and first level by ordering things on the basis of a fore-understanding that expresses interests and emotions, and that inherits a language, a culture, and historical forms of rationality. Things appear, are given as entities, and "come to Being" only within the horizon of a project, otherwise they might not stand forth from their background and from one another. Therefore, hermeneutics can also be defined as a Kantianism passed through the existentialistic experience of finitude and thus of historicity. A transformation at whose root stands the existential analytic of *Being and Time*, which in its turn inherited many elements from pragmatism (things are first of all and in most cases instruments and, for this reason, are given only in a project), elements that much of today's realism tends to set aside without ever really discussing.

Does hermeneutics have the right, thus—however summarily—defined, to claim to express the "spirit of the times," to put itself forward as the *koiné* of the recent decades of Western culture? There is likely no aspect of what is called the postmodern world that is not marked by the pervasive nature of interpretation. Its features can be recalled in a brief list: the diffusion of mass media, which not too paradoxically develops the vague and general awareness of their character as interpretative agents neither neutral nor "objective"; the self-awareness of historiography, for which even the idea of history is a rhetorical scheme, that nonetheless can no longer count as the principle of reality to which was entrusted the major part of modern philosophy after and as an alternative to the empiricist and positivist faith in the facts acquired through sensation and experimentation; the rise of the multiplicity of cultures, which, through the persistence of their own rules, deny a unitary and progressive idea of rationality; the psychoanalytical destruction of faith in the finality of consciousness; and so on, by listing all the way to the theory of paradigms ripened in the very self-consciousness of scientists.

I am not claiming in a contradictory manner that hermeneutics, summed up in Nietzsche's maxim, is the most adequate description of late-modern culture. Instead, I argue that it is the most reasonable interpretation of it. That it is an interpretation means that one consciously formulates it within the framework of a project—a thrown project, according to Heidegger's terminology. Therefore, it is recognized as the reasonable interpretation in view of a telos that chooses how much, and in what measure, it is already committed, because it belongs there in a historical-destinal way. Neither the idea of reason, nor reasonability, on the basis of which hermeneutics wants to be judged, nor the specific arguments that it can put forward to verify it in light of this criterion are external to its specific historical condition, to its destiny. Would this be a symptom of the sinking into irrationalism, to the relativism of Weltanschauungen, generally demonized because at its base it predicts the violent struggle of all against all, a sort of return to the primal state? As I tried to show in *Beyond Interpretation*, hermeneutics presents itself as pure and dangerous relativism only if it does not take its own nihilistic implications seriously enough, since the "truth of hermeneutics" as an alternative theory to others (and first of all to the concept of truth as the "reflection" of "facts") cannot be legitimated by its claim to count as the description equal to a state of things that is metaphysically fixed (there are no facts, there are only interpretations), but must also recognize that, as an interpretation itself, its only possibility is that of arguing about itself as such, that is, as an internal "description" or reading sui generis of the historical condition into which it is thrown and that chooses to be oriented in a definite direction, for which there are no other criteria except for those it inherits, by interpreting, from that same origin. Now, the origin understood as legitimization of the truth of hermeneutics can only be presented in light of nihilism; only a Being that proceeds, indefinitely (and not *infinitely*), toward its own weakening legitimates the validation of the idea of truth as interpretation and not as correspondence. If it were not this way, hermeneutics would only be a metaphysical-descriptive theory of the irreducible plurality of cultures; and as metaphysical-descriptive, it would still be the victim, and this time in an untenable way, of a performative self-contradiction—untenable because such self-contradiction refutes precisely, and perhaps above all, whoever pretends that the true is correspondence to the state of things.

To take notice of the pervasiveness of interpretation in postmodern culture, and to try to think this awareness also as an interpretation and not as a new relativistic metaphysics, means engaging the responsibility of moving in a direction, by knowing ourselves to be from somewhere, conditioned, historical. In this perspective, whoever defends the right to realism, or of metaphysics as the conscious and practical reflection of the objective truth of Being, is an interlocutor as "interpreting" as anyone else. They are doing hermeneutics but do not know it, one could say with Molière. Such a person interprets in view of a project that he nevertheless does not recognize as such because he believes he is motivated by the pure will to truth as the reflection of the structure of things "out there." The good reasons for choosing the hermeneutician over the realist, but also over the metaphysical relativist, or against the metaphysician tout court, are entrusted to the rational preferability of the project that inspires the interpretation of its provenance. We can begin with the fact that project and interpretation come to be recognized as such by the hermeneutician and are explicitly put into play. On the other hand, the metaphysician—whether realist, relativist, or naturalist—is always the one who believes he is (able to be) speaking from no standpoint, who does account for (or put into play) himself in his picture of consciousness, and he is therefore—yes he—exposed to the devastating effect of the performative self-contradiction.

The metaphysician's will to truth begins by accepting as obvious that the latter might signify the objective reflection of the state of things, and that this reflection might be possible and desirable as the final value for consciousness and action. Even in a language that is not as clearly hermeneutic as Heidegger's, for example, from the point of view of Habermas's theory of communicative action, one could say that here there is a "colonizing" generalization of all the spheres of action, beginning with strategic action: one can certainly recognize that to know how things stand in a certain environment is necessary and useful with some end in view; but how much to this end—insofar as from the last one we can no longer think it as means to some other—certainly is not worth being referred to truth as correspondence, and it is inevitably sent back to the project. A project that has as its ultimate value the reflection of those things as they are, that, for example, thinks that the emancipation of humanity or even, more modestly, the happiness or fulfillment of the individual consists in the consciousness of the objective truth, incurs all of the objections—and real contradictions—facing every theory that does not take stock of historicity, first and foremost its own.

Against the rational preferability of hermeneutics—let us repeat it, from the point of view of a notion of rationality that lets itself be grasped interpretatively within its own provenance—are opposed, on the side of realism in its various forms, whether logical-metaphysical reasons (the self-contradictory nature of nihilism) or fundamentally those that only have the appearance of being definitive, motivations less abstract and nevertheless tied to historical and pragmatic demands. Now, even though hermeneutic ontology, in the name of historical experience and the spirit of the times, cannot pay attention to the antiskeptical argument that claims to be victorious, it is still sensitive to those objections that are referred back to these very sources.

To push away hermeneutics as nihilistic ontology seems necessary, in the first place, because the validity of the experimental sciences of nature would end up being undermined. Here I am using the term "validity" in a broad and generic sense, as the opposite of invalidity—in reference both to logic and to the capacity of being respected also, and perhaps above all, in the "conflict of the faculties"—and as hegemonic knowledge to which one grants a guiding function for collective life. The greater number of the choices that are presented in contemporary philosophical debates, and first of all those that, only for schematic convenience, can be referred back to the opposition between "Analytics" and "Continentals," have at stake the validity, in this general sense, of the experimental sciences. Hermeneutic nihilism seems to threaten this validity insofar as it comes to be identified, as was seen arbitrarily, with a relativistic metaphysics, which would also and above all have as its consequence the putting at risk of the practical and social authority of science. This risk is all the more feared the more the cultural pluralism of advanced industrial societies entails the possible diffusion of a chaotic scientific and technological pluralism, with effects that pose grave questions of social and political importance. One thinks about how one decides which medical treatments are used or even paid for by the various national health services.

Hermeneutics, both with its nihilistic ontology and above all with reference to the historicity of forms of knowledge (their involvement with the distribution of social power, their comprehensive and not disinterested character), would produce (according to their critics) the dangerous outcome of the delegitimization of science, along with (and more seriously) the delegitimization of morality. In other terms, one can even discuss methodological anarchism in restricted circles of epistemologists and scientists; but, when it becomes a sort of shared feeling, and it is spread, for example, beyond the academic circles through the work of deconstruction by the many critics inspired by Derrida, the principle of reality is robustly defended, namely, the not purely historical validity of propositions ascertained through science.

But methodological anarchism, to be exact, is not an expression invented by nihilistic hermeneutics; it originates in the realm of those philosophers considered respectful of science and its realism, at least as a matter of principle. The fact is that a nihilistic ontology seems nevertheless to be the shared result of both the analytic and the continental tradition, at least to the degree that the latter can be identified with hermeneutics. To list the aspects of contemporary culture of which nihilism can be presented as the "adequate" interpretation, one includes not only the mediatization of society, the pluralism of cultures, the Freudian denial of the finality of consciousness, and the secularization of religion and of power, but also and above all the "irrealistic" developments of the sciences and epistemologies that accompany it. Take, for example, an excerpt from *Reason, Truth and History* by Hilary Putnam (1981), a philosopher from the analytic tradition: "*What objects does the world consist of?* is a question that only makes sense to ask within a theory or description"; truth "is some sort of rational acceptability and not correspondence with mind-independent or discourse-independent 'states of affairs.'"[1] It is, as is known, what Putnam calls "internal realism" or internalist perspective—opposed to the externalist perspective of "metaphysical realism," according to which "the world consists of some fixed totality of mind-independent objects. There is exactly one true and complete description of 'the way the world is.' Truth involves some sort of correspondence relation between words or thought-signs and external things and sets of things."[2] Who knows if Putnam thinks that this internalist thesis is an exact description (and thus "externalist") of the way things are? We ought to suppose, assuming that it is not terribly incoherent, that even he would argue for the rational acceptability of his thesis on the basis of the calls to the sort of vague and impressionistic experience referred to by hermeneutics.

Even the most dogmatic metaphysical realism lacks the possibility of some crucial experiment that would "realistically" prove a thesis, because every delimitation of the realm of importance is always already an interpretative act; for good reason, an internal realism like Putnam's can with some difficulty escape from the drift, or from the real historicistic unfounding and its nihilistic implications.[3] Certainly, the internal realism of Putnam is not the only outcome of analytic and postanalytic epistemology, and not even perhaps a dominant theoretical position in that realm. Together with many other aspects of this tradition (for certain aspects there is Strawson, and Thomas Kuhn's theory of paradigms ripens and is widespread first of all in the analytic realm, but one can also cite the falsificationism of Popper, which, in spite of every reading to the contrary, is not a "realist" theory, and Popper has always been an influential interlocutor with analytical epistemologists), it, however, at least shows a certain reasonability of the thesis according to which the nihilistic ontology of hermeneutics has good qualifications for presenting itself as the *koiné* of the culture of our age.

If (as one could show more broadly) hermeneutic nihilism does not threaten science any more than many epistemological theories considered friendlier and more attentive to its rules, what remains of the realist polemic against hermeneutics? In line with the fundamental convictions of hermeneuticians, according to whom every defense of truth is moved by a project, which is moved by an interest, one needs to ask about the demands that motivate this polemic.

What is there at the root of the need to speak of reality as something substantial, in the expression of Putnam, as a "fixed totality of mind-independent objects"? If we consider the "temptation of realism" in its aspects of being a new way of doing philosophy, we can track down a certain number of contingent motivations, not to be undervalued but probably not exhaustive: the banal generational revolt against hermeneutics that, as *koiné*, is by now a paradigm that is established although variegated; the fundamentalist neurosis that follows the late-industrial society as the regressive reaction of defense against the postmodern Babel of languages and values, that is, realism as the possible ideology of the silent majority, or simply, among certain academic philosophers, the call to order of a philosophy that according to them ought to return to being, as in the times of prevailing positivism and neo-Kantianism, (quasi-)positive research on the mechanisms of understanding; the return to Kant against the "Hegelian" *lignée*; cognitive sciences. Enough epochal chatter; let us return to deal with how we know the world, beginning with sensation. (And naturally and "realistically," philosophy as special science, which does not discuss its own delimitation but stands within it with productivity.)

These motivations are not far-fetched, but also not exhaustive. A conclusion, here, still ought to be the following: (a) to show further that hermeneutics is not at all empirical idealism, which not for nothing dreams of placing in doubt the "passivity" of sensibility, to use Kantian terminology; (b) that to speak, for this "passivity," of the reception of messages rather than of the encounter with objects or of the registration of impressions on the tabula rasa of the mind endangers neither the pursuit of scientific consciousness nor one's firm grounding in daily life, in the relations with others, and so on.

Since here I am referring to only the first movements of a *work in progress* on the concept of reality, I will limit myself to highlighting these two concluding themes by insisting on the fact that the analysis of experience conducted by Heidegger in *Being and Time* is of great value to hermeneutic ontology, that it was a pragmaticist analysis, but certainly not a Berkeleian one. To follow the second Heidegger, the Heidegger of the nihilistic ontology of the event, does not at all abandon the originarily phenomenological awareness of experience as the encounter with the other by itself. The existential analytic, if ever, brings to phenomenology the indispensible opening onto the historical dimension of the encounter. Nietzsche's maxim "this too is an interpretation" is not tantamount to reestablishing the difference between things in themselves and the cognitive schemata that Husserl already, and later, among others, Davidson, had rightly set aside. That in respect to which interpretation is "only" an interpretation is not the world out there as the fixed totality of the objects independent of my consciousness, but the inheritance of other interpretations in their turn inseparable from what was given to them as object. It is not surprising that Heidegger calls this very handing down of interpretations (inseparable from the facts that they understand) the "history of Being." Even the appeal to the objectivity of things as they are in themselves matters only insofar as it is a thesis by some person against some other, namely, insofar as it is an interpretation motivated by projects, anticipations, and interests (in the better sense of the word). Reality "itself" does not speak by itself; it needs a spokesperson—that is, to be precise, motivated interpreters who decide how to represent on a map a territory to which they have had access through more ancient maps.

If one abandons the idea of cognitive schemata opposed to the world as a fixed totality of independent objects, it becomes clear that the passivity of the experience of the world is provenance (being thrown, not beginning from zero, by itself, and so on) rather than the receptivity of sense organs that are always "objectively" equal. That reality is (our) history does not turn it into a fable, for if the true world has become a fable, as Nietzsche writes, by that very act the fable (the cognitive schema that ought to reduce everything to itself) is also negated. From this point, it seems, a hermeneutic recovery of "reality" can begin.

THE GIFFORD LECTURES

5

TARSKI AND THE
QUOTATION MARKS

P lease allow me to begin with an autobiographical reference, to my past and my present, as a believing or half-believing Christian—a reference that is, however, not at all out of place in a context where theology has its role. "*Redemisti nos Domine, Deus veritatis*"—it is a phrase from the Latin breviary, the book of hours, one that I have repeated many times. The emphasis rests on the term *veritas*, which has always characterized much of the history of philosophy, of theology, and of religious experience. Is it possible that the *veritas* of which this passage speaks, and that, especially when it is associated with the name of God, has the power to redeem us, is the same one defined by Tarski's principle? "It is raining" is true if, and only if, it is raining. This question, or, if one prefers, this paradox, best summarizes my more recent philosophical work that has earned me the honor of this invitation. I am well aware of the importance of this occasion when I think of the names of the philosophers who have given the Gifford Lectures, which I have always viewed more or less as a Nobel Prize of Philosophy.

The reflections that I intend to develop concerning the "end of reality" begin with this very paradox about the notion of truth. I would not be able to say to what extent this is an "objective" reconstruction of the itinerary that has led me to my—provisional—conclusions about

reality, Being, and the meaning of existence. These are also the traditional themes of every philosophical meditation, more or less those
that Kant condensed in his three famous questions: What can I know?
What ought I to do? What can I hope? However, I must say that today
it really seems to me that there is a linear development from the discovery of the Heideggerian critique of the metaphysical conception of
truth—the correspondence between *intellectus* and *res*—to the idea of
the weakening of the Being of entities as the only possible philosophy
of history and theory of emancipation.

The importance of the *quotation marks* has already been emphasized many times in philosophical discourse. I will recall here only the
important reflection that Jacques Derrida conducted on the critical
edition of the works of Nietzsche that contained the comment "I have
forgotten my umbrella." Certainly, there are examples of similar annotations, references to banal aspects of daily life, in Kant's *Opus posthu-
mum*. However, if I am not wrong, in that case it was not a question
of *quotation marks*, but only a matter of annotations unduly mixed
with comments of a more philosophical nature. Nevertheless, I do
not intend to linger here on Derrida's Nietzschean reflections; the reference serves only as an example, and also as an occasion to honor a
friend and teacher who generated many of the spurs that have led me to
the conclusions under discussion.

So, why do the *quotation marks* in Tarski's principle warrant so much
attention in our present discussion? I know well that there have been
many debates about this principle, and I do not intend, or perhaps I
would not know how, to take them up here. I will begin only by remembering another friend and teacher who is gone, Richard Rorty, who,
in dialogue with Pascal Engel in *What's the Use of Truth?*,[1] claims not
to be interested in the argument over realism and antirealism that still
engages part of contemporary philosophy. The argument, namely, over
the meaning one can attribute to Tarski's famous principle, according
to which "P" is true if and only if P. Translated, that means: "it is raining" is true if and only if it is raining. The quotation marks are crucial,

obviously—or not very obviously, outside of the realm of interlocutors interested in this debate. Indeed, as Rorty's example shows, Tarski's famous principle can be for many, not only for laymen but also for the philosopher, just one more proof of the uselessness of a certain type of philosophy.

But prior to the argument over its utility, Tarski's principle confronts a problem that is still more radical: Does the second P really stand outside of quotation marks? Who says such a thing? Above all else, the response to this question helps delineate the answer to Rorty's question about the usefulness or uselessness of the principle. Whoever says, claims, or affirms that P should stand outside of quotation marks is probably somebody who benefits from its being stated in this way. His affirmation must also be placed between quotation marks. The reason usually put forward for accepting that the second P stands outside of quotation marks is that, otherwise, a large part of our discourses about the true, the false, justified and unjustified claims, the rationality or irrationality of our behavior, and political and ethical decisions would be for naught—they would not in their own right make any sense. Every time that we challenge a thesis, that we claim something against something else, we use the distinction between "P" and P. The argument in favor of Tarski's principle, therefore, is that we need this principle. But yet again: who needs it? And, above all, such an argument contrary to Rorty's pragmatic "relativism" is clearly self-contradictory. Tarski's thesis ought to be accepted only because it is true, not because it is said by or to a specific listener, namely, the "we" (of shared experience) that is required to demonstrate its validity.

As we see, here we are wrapped up in a series of questions that seem to find no conclusion at all, or that can be avoided only if one rejects the question "who says it?" But this is the question that cannot be avoided, it seems, unless one wants to exclude it through an authoritarian prohibition, with an action that for certain is very unphilosophical.

The question, as one will know, is one that Nietzsche brutally resolves by writing that "there are no facts, only interpretations. And this too is an interpretation." Whoever suggests that we accept Tarski's thesis also claims that we cannot do without it if we have to explain our shared experience. But our shared experience—that which is also called "the greatest evidence available here and now"—is an interpretation. We tend not to call it an interpretation only to distinguish it from more markedly individual opinions, which we often say are "only" interpretations. But wouldn't a good positivist also say that there are no facts unless they are ascertained, experienced, recognized by someone as such? And what of the history of the earth before the appearance of humans? If we speak of it, we are obviously situating it within a framework; if not, it is as if it never was. But we suffer its consequences, the effects it has on us, even if we know nothing of it; therefore, it is something real, prior to and outside of our discourse about it. Certainly it is; but as it is reflected in us, it is already in some sense "relative" (in relation) to us.

But does justifying the interpretative character of every truth claim mean that there are no things unless we invent them (empirical idealism)? Or that the order in which they appear is an order established by us, more or less arbitrarily (a sort of subjectivistic-transcendental idealism)? Kant, who is not at all a dead dog, claims that we cannot know the things in themselves, but only those that appear phenomenally within the scope of our a priori (time, space, categories). Therefore, should we say that every distinction between mere idle talk and "true" propositions ought to be erased? If we say that the difference between true and false is always a difference between more or less shared and acceptable interpretations, we hold this very same distinction; and we have no need to imagine a fact that "exists" outside of every human apprehension.

Who is not satisfied by this solution? To what, or to whom, is "truth" without quotation marks useful? Perhaps, as someone suggests,[2] it might serve to place the existing order under question—enlightenment and revolution, human rights against totalitarianism, the progress of knowledge against obscurantism. But really? Let's not forget that the church, and often also princes and governments, had always thundered against Kant and his perverse subjectivism. Certainly, this would not be a "proof" from the point of view of a Tarskian. Let's take it only as a "sign" that reminds us to pay attention. But are we discovering a "truth" about truth? Will we say "it is true" that Tarski's thesis is useful to whomever possesses the power to impose his own interpretation as the only true one? No; as good pragmatists, maybe with a smattering of Marx's critique of ideology, we will only say that it is what sounds "to us" like truth—what is able to set us free. We cannot ever pretend to have a God's-eye point of view. We can only recognize that we see things according to certain prejudices, to certain interests, and if the truth is ever possible, it is the result of an agreement that is necessitated not by any definitive evidence, but only by charity, by solidarity, by the human (all too human?) need to live in agreement with others.

Moreover, if you ask a realist "Tarskian" why one ought to acknowledge that "it is raining" when it is raining, he will refer you again to shared experience: yours, of getting wet, and that of the others, who agree with the same description: namely, "the greatest evidence available at the moment." But that everyone turns to you and agrees that it is raining—wouldn't that be the effect of a shared interpretation? "Everyone" means those to whom we can in fact address the question— by going against Popper's well-known objections about the value of induction. This would be the meaning of the phrase "the greatest evidence available at this moment." That does not allow us to say without doubt, beyond any objection, that it really is raining. In the end, we can only say that the facts are precisely *fatti* (literally, "made") by someone, or *dati* (*principium reddendae rationis*), literally "given" to whomever wishes to examine them and "use" them for a discussion. Even the hyperbolic thesis, according to which one ought to conclude that a fact not ascertained by me or by anyone else does not "exist," has a very limited importance. When I say, however, that the fact must exist, I am only saying it is possible that I myself or some other can verify it in the future, but nothing more. If not, the question returns to the thing in itself, which I can always think, but never verify phenomenally, and about which, therefore, I can no longer say, as the Tarskian would like, that it "exists" independently of me.

The experimental knowledge of reality on which scientific propositions are founded, and which implies the repeatability of the experiment by anyone else, is also a strong argument in favor of my thesis about interpretation. The "objectivity" of the phenomenon that it describes consists in the repeatability of the experiment by other researchers. The presence of a method and the use of sophisticated instruments, however, do not distinguish this repetition of experiences in any essential way from those of shared everyday life: one always deals with other subjects who are asked to confirm or deny a particular interpretation of events. But exactly, events "as such" *are* such only because they can be experienced repeatedly. Would this also be one of the meanings of the Aristotelian expression *to ti en einai*, what Being *was*?

Should we be shocked by the "element of chance" that is thus introduced in the very notion of "reality"? It would be a scandal like the one caused by pragmatism: what is true is therefore only what is good for us as individuals or as a group? Pragmatism is shocking, and probably philosophically (that is, pragmatically) unacceptable, only if it is not formulated as historicism (*to ti en einai*, exactly). The crucial argument by Tarskians—let's use this name a bit loosely—is this: if "there were" no rain, the real fact beyond our verification, we could no longer speak or argue. As often occurs in the case of radical empiricism, this is a solipsistic argument: if there is no fact outside of me, there is only I who would absurdly pretend to determine reality itself (once again, however, the absurd would rest in the fact that reality must be "external"). But my interpretation is not born from zero, and has nothing to do with the encounter of a "subject" with an "object" in a one-to-one relation. As in the case of givenness as the repeatability of the experiment, I am not an isolated subject: I speak a language, I use a vocabulary and therefore a syntax and a set of criteria for validity. In short, what gives "reality" to the facts that I interpret is the history into which

I have been placed. The objects—a Marxist would say—are crystallized social relations.

Would a similar interpretation be enough to satisfy the problems of "argumentability" raised by the realists? The risk that they indicate, and with reason if one begins with their solipsistic presuppositions, is that there would be no way to place shared beliefs into discussion: there is a canon of shared interpretation, this is what we call reality—and therefore, to what should we appeal in order to declare our disagreement, maybe even in order to "correct" errors and violations of "rights"?

The Kantian distinction between noumenon and phenomenon is useful here when integrated with Heidegger's famous affirmation that "science does not think." For us this means there is always enough light to distinguish a true proposition from a false one, at least if we refer to truths "of fact" that are such because they are formulated according to available criteria, something that Thomas Kuhn would call "normal science," in the realm of which problems are resolved by using accepted paradigms that are not subjected to critique. If we remain within the realm of phenomena, Kant would say, one can always establish that something is true and that something is false. Not even Kant, however, was thinking that one could apply this discourse to philosophy; there is no scientific discourse about the noumenal and of those "things" that belong to it, such as freedom, the existence of God, and the world in its totality. One can always correct an error in terms of truths "of fact" by applying the paradigms in use. It is so also for the justification of a right, when one can refer to a code in force, or for the clarification of the meaning of a dogmatic truth when one accepts the authority of the church. But in all of these cases it is not that "there is" something "out there," as Rorty would say. We always move within paradigms and fore-understandings that coincide with what we call "reality." But why at a certain point, in certain moments, do some of us raise the problem of facts *vs.* interpretations?

This is, by the way, a question that the "Tarskians" do not consider willingly, or, better, that they solve by bringing it right back to the distinction between truth and error, such that the question they pose to hermeneutic thinkers—how can you oppose an error if not in the name of a truth?—turns back against them. How can you critique the paradigms in use if they are the only ones on the basis of which you can claim to be able to make your distinctions? The "reactionary" nature of the realism à la Tarski depends on this reductive acceptance of the notion of truth, whatever may be the critical intentions of its proponents.

But again why, and when, does the problem of facts *vs.* interpretations arise? It is not surprising that the history of hermeneutics is profoundly intertwined with the entire history of modern Europe. Even before the Protestant Reformation took on its radically political meaning, the question of interpretation had already for some time begun to place in doubt the definitive nature of the paradigms in use and their authority: even the problem of how to read in ethically correct ways the often dishonest and suspect behavior of Homer's gods was a problem of socially enforced paradigms, if one thinks of the pedagogical function that belonged to the Homeric poems; and obviously this discourse is still more relevant for the ways of reading the sacred Scripture theorized and debated by medieval hermeneutics. If one reflects on these examples, it also becomes clear that the problem of interpretation does not really "arise" in determinate moments; it always accompanies the debate over the paradigms in use, it represents in them an intimate critical vocation that is activated in diverse ways above all in relation to social and political facts. Luther did not begin preaching the liberal examination of Scripture only to meet the demand born in theoretical reflection: he wanted to rebel against the papacy and against the corrupt condition into which the church of that time had fallen. Did this have anything to do with the society of his time? It is not so arbitrary to think that he had at heart the sorts of poor who are exploited in every way, especially in the name of religious motivations. Certainly, he was a monk and therefore one could expect that he would not have had motives for rebelling against a condition of privilege that he himself enjoyed. It is clear that the sociological "explanation" of his revolt cannot be pushed ahead very far, if not for risking the absurdity of a simplistic determinism. But since we are looking for the reasons why the crisis of a paradigm develops (in Kuhn, the example is always the end of the Ptolemaic paradigm in favor of the Copernican, which cannot be explained through a comparison between the two, since it would require a metaparadigm as the basis for the evaluation), we can think that in Luther there was at work a mechanism analogous to that which is encountered in the rather general tendency of social critique by "humanistic" intellectuals in respect to scientific ones. Can we speak provocatively of a "noumenal marginality" for this phenomenon? A definition that is not too paradoxical, which perhaps translates the revolutionary vocation of Marx's proletariat only in "Kantian" language? For whatever this reference is worth, it is in the end clear that the crisis of a theoretical paradigm, even the Ptolemaic one, is not exclusive to theory but involves, more than we tend to believe, the events of the social subjects, individuals, and groups who are concerned with them.

Here we are not following a divergent path in respect to the center of our discourse. To pose the question of why and how the problem of facts *vs.* interpretations is born is also a way of responding to our main question: how is a critical attitude possible that does not appeal to the difference between "objective" truth and error?

Or more precisely: what still remains of "truth" in the position I am defending? Let's try to think of truth in terms of "noumenal marginality" (or simply of the history of Being). This refers not only to the Marxist idea of the revolutionary proletariat, but also to the phrase from the Gospel according to which "the truth will set you free."

If we do not think we are able to argue solely and principally in reference to "how things are," because we think that the way they are one way or another is also the effect of interpretation, namely, that every truth about them is what is "good for" someone, the problem of reasoning becomes a question of choice.

If one raises the question of the difference between facts and interpretations, it is because one is not at ease with the paradigms in use. We do not feel at one with the group, in society, with the pursuits shared by "everyone" but not by us. So, are we not at ease with Tarski's simple proposition? If it rains, the thing has the same meaning for us as for "everyone" who lives alongside us. In fact the question of the validity of paradigms does not arise with the problem of the rain. It does not arise from truths of fact, what for Kant would be topics for the science of phenomena. The questions that break the paradigm are "noumenal": values, ethics, ways of organizing social life, the general meaning of life. And the break occurs right when someone suggests that the reasonable way to deal with such questions is by reducing them to the level of truths of fact and searching for their solution with the methods of science. Admittedly, we have placed ourselves on slippery ground. What places us at odds with the Tarskians is the very idea of the paradigm and of its historicity. But once we admit that the paradigm is historical and not "natural," how do we move forward? Namely, what "truth" do we suggest in place of Tarski's principle, or at least in place of its claim of general value?

Let's begin from zero. Presented with the thesis that "it is raining" is true only if it is in fact raining, we can object that the second "it is raining" should also be placed between quotation marks: there is a community that admits the existence of a certain reality to which it refers in order to decide what is true and what is false. On our part, we still ask who comprises this community of "everyone." The question of the truth of "it is raining" becomes a question of negotiation with the community that professes and applies the paradigm. It is as if, by reflecting on a truth as elementary as "it is raining," we discover that we are historical beings and that "the greatest evidence available at the moment" is constructed only with an agreement that can be placed under scrutiny and renegotiated.[3] Whatever "is," of which we predicate "being," is not always and in any case, but occurs within a play of interpersonal relations. If we take note that the affirmation of a truth also reflects a certain hierarchy of social power, does it or does it not any longer make sense to hold on to the thesis of truth as the correspondence of the proposition to the thing? Even the "taking note" that it "makes sense" can withstand the obvious objection of the Tarskians: aren't we putting forward truths of fact as arguments? Sure, but neither the taking note nor, above all, recognizing that something makes sense are things analogous to the "it is raining" of Tarski.

What we are saying is one of the ways of claiming that if "there is" something like the "external" reality of the Tarskians, it is only the whole of the interpretations shared and canonized in a certain society and in a determinate historical moment. To propose a different sociohistorical order, even beginning from the dissatisfaction with certain aspects of the paradigm in use, certainly cannot be done with "cogent" arguments of the ostensive sort—"I will show you that"—but only with edifying words: "Don't you feel that it would be better if . . . " Let us say that here we are rediscovering the Kant of the *Critique of Judgment* as an indispensable basis for the Kant of the *Critique of Pure Reason*.

We all know that Richard Rorty spoke about philosophy as an "edifying" discourse rather than an apodictic discourse in his famous book *Philosophy and the Mirror of Nature*. In that book, he even had the courage—and in those years it took much more than today—to point to Dewey, Heidegger, and Wittgenstein as the three decisive philosophers of the twentieth century. Today, in many realms of philosophy—Anglo-American no less than Continental—it seems that these three figures have been forgotten in favor of a new "realism" that risks falling back into the idea of the mirroring of nature that Rorty wanted to liquidate, and that also has significant and dangerous consequences in terms of social and political life. To be antirealists today is perhaps the only way to still be "revolutionary."

6

BEYOND PHENOMENOLOGY

n order to understand the sense of a philosophical position, as I learned from one of my teachers at the University of Turin, one needs to understand the positions against which it has been articulated, or even to reconstruct the basic problem that it is trying to solve. These ideas are only variations of the Hegelian (but also, more remotely, Aristotelian) conception of the experience of truth: truth is only that which assumes and sublates in itself the opposing thesis by constructing a synthesis that *hebt auf* what at the beginning was presented as its opposite. Much more than the correct description of that which happens "outside of the quotation marks," truth is here the experience of change that happens in the dialectical exchange with what in Hegelian terms is called the antithesis. It is true that the change under discussion here is not independent of the fact of becoming aware that it really is raining "out there" beyond the quotation marks. However, as will be seen from the discussion that began with Tarski's principle, the true is only the change that happens in the one who has the experience of "raining." It does not involve any claim about the "state of the world" outside of the quotations. Popper's falsificationism can also be easily reduced to a theory of ad hominem arguments: to falsify a proposition says nothing about the state of the world; it convinces us only that one cannot think that P is the case.

Let's leave Popper and his logic alone. What I intend to discuss today under the title that alludes to phenomenology is both a historical reconstruction—Heidegger of the 1920s—and the reasons that we have, according to me, for declaring ourselves antirealists. By now it is obvious that the conclusion I reached in the preceding lecture cannot be summed up in a proposition such as "It is true that Tarski's principle is not valid." In logical terms (bah!) it would be: "not-P" is true if and only if not-P. But I do not want to venture into these formalisms, which as you already know are completely foreign to me. I will thus continue to "recount" my position in everyday language. I began with the autobiographical allusion to my relation with the term *veritas*, and along with this reference to the Hegelian vision of the true as the synthesis and *Aufhebung* of the opposite position, one will understand how I intend to connect *veritas* with the *redemptio* I spoke about when I cited the Latin breviary. Here neither I nor (*si licet*) Heidegger in the early decades of the twentieth century when he was preparing and published *Sein und Zeit* critique the Tarskian idea of a world "out there" because it seems, "in reality," that "there is not" a world out there. Ultimately, I am well aware that my talk risks the only antiskeptical objection: if you say there is no truth, you nonetheless claim to speak a truth, and so on. It is not in the name of a superior realism (the demonstrative awareness that "there is not" a world out there) that one can and one must reject Tarski's principle and his realistic metaphysics. The reasons for assuming an antirealist position are in many ways analogous—or indeed equal, but in a different phase of historical development—to those that compelled Heidegger, at the beginning of the last century, to reject the notion of truth as *adaequatio rei et intellectus*. Neither his reasons nor ours today can return to the purpose of describing the same notion of truth in a way more adequate and true. It is clear: Heidegger in his time and we here and now are well aware of still using, in many situations, the grammar and syntax of "objective" truth. In this, one finds the unyielding force of Tarski's principle: just by saying this, as we know, I also use a "descriptive" way of speaking. And it is so if I seek to reconstruct the historical situation of Heidegger in the 1920s. And with this? Nietzsche would say, "And this too is an interpretation"— but to set it aside because it is "only" an interpretation is possible only if one presumes that Tarski's principle is valid in any case, if, namely, it is posited primarily in a realistic point of view that is precisely under question. And nevertheless, this Nietzschean (and also Heideggerian) response is not in any case a "winner's argument" that ought to bring the battle against the realists to a victorious end. One of the principle teachings of Heidegger is contained in the notion, rather mysterious from the point of view of the literal meaning of the term, of *Verwindung*, which means recovering from an illness by preserving its vestiges, resigning oneself to something from which one cannot be set totally free, and even, in my view, distortion, twisting. Faced with the language of realistic metaphysics, from which we strain to exit, we always have only the possibility of a *Verwindung*. We cannot really overcome it (*Überwinden*) because this would involve the adoption of an alternative metaphysics that would place us back in the "realistic" condition that we wanted to leave behind.

Sure. But why, I will ask again, do we want to leave realistic metaphysics behind? The path of *Verwindung* is imposed by the impossibility of completely abandoning a metaphysics without falling into a new one: "if you say that everything is false, you still claim that this proposition is true." Here one is reminded, even if it originates in a very distant situation, of the passage from Walter Benjamin about what inspired the revolutionaries in their struggle to destroy the old order: "they are nourished by the image of enslaved ancestors rather than that of liberated grandchildren."[1] And let us remember Montale: "we can only say this today: what we are not is what we do not want—of whom?" In the antirealism that inspires my lecture today, as with (and motivated by) the antirealism of Heidegger in *Sein und Zeit*, the image of enslaved forefathers is especially decisive, namely, the perception of the ethico-political, let us say existential, consequences of metaphysical realism. Very simply, in order to reconstruct, to rethink historically (not *historisch*, Heidegger would say, but *geschichtlich*), the reasons why Heidegger understood the project of going "beyond phenomenology" as his proper philosophical vocation, it is necessary to understand both the weight of his gesture back then and the multiple dimensions of our efforts today.

We know that in 1927, the year *Sein und Zeit* was published, Heidegger's falling out with his teacher Husserl took shape in all of its gravity. And the theme of the dispute, brought to maturity above all in the (failed) collaboration between Husserl and his disciple over the article "Phenomenology" in the *Encyclopedia Britannica*, was fundamental ontology. Husserl up to that point had operated in a realm that was greatly affected by the atmosphere of neo-Kantianism dominating the German universities at that time. It is true that the ideal of going "to the things themselves" appeared more realistic than Kantian and neo-Kantian transcendentalism, but in the end the so-called regional ontologies, to which he wanted to add fundamental ontology as a foundation, were nothing more than a determination of the various "regions" in which the world of objects is given to the Kantian transcendental subject. The differences between the remembered, the willed, the imagined, the experienced in flesh and bone, and the like were in the final analysis nothing more than this.

For Husserl, naturally, the legitimacy of talking about ontology with regard to these distinctions originated directly from what for him was the decisive "discovery" of phenomenology, namely, the fact that in the eidetic intuition both the specific object and the *eidos* are given, in fact the *eide* that are inseparably constituted in Being. From this point of view, one can even ask why a fundamental ontology is still necessary. Or at least, it becomes very understandable that philosophy is reduced to regional ontologies. It is very probable that for Husserl, or at least for Husserl before the *Krisis*, the regional ontologies really could exhaust all of philosophy. Although it is not entirely clear from the correspondences he exchanged with Heidegger during the time when he was writing the article for the *Encyclopedia Britannica*, it is very likely that the disagreement between the master and his disciple dealt precisely with these themes. At least, this is how the dispute and the falling out are understood today. We must also remember the project that Husserl expressed in the famous page from his diary in 1906, when he wrote that life was not bearable unless he could hope to achieve clarity and "an inner solidity" (September 25, 1906). There was a sort of religious need on that page (confirmed also by the conclusion that speaks of "seeing the promised land"). But can the regional ontologies, and their reference to the transcendental "I," really satisfy this need? If we want to sum this all up in simple and yet accurate terms—the difference between Husserl and Heidegger during the time when the former was developing phenomenology and the latter was writing *Sein und Zeit*—we can rightly speak of a scientific-mathematical mind versus an intensely religious spirit. The profound ethical meaning that Husserl gave to his phenomenological work can also be read easily as a dedication to a task that is not criticized as such. As in the case of the regional ontologies, Husserl did not criticize the legitimacy of the traditional division of intellectual work; the task that he took on is not unlike that taken on by the neo-Kantians of the time, the transcendental foundation of the specific spheres of experience, the distinction of which he did not question.

The dissatisfaction (ours and probably Heidegger's) with the way that the "mathematical" Husserl develops his plan of achieving an inner solidity, stopping at the transcendental foundation of the regional ontologies, is very similar to what Heidegger expresses in his review of Jaspers's *Psychologie der Weltanschauungen*, written in 1919 but not published until 1976 in *Wegmarken*. In that review, Heidegger criticizes Jaspers for having forgotten the purpose he set forth in the book's introduction, which was to study the Weltanschauungen in order to question his own. Instead of completing this task, in Heidegger's view, Jaspers only attempted to construct a substantially aesthetic panorama, that is, in Heidegger's words, a purely descriptive and objective one of the various types of worldviews.

Briefly, if we look at *Sein und Zeit*, which Heidegger published in 1927, the very same year that he quarreled with his teacher over the encyclopedia article, the essential need at the core of fundamental ontology is precisely that which is announced in the first few pages of the book, namely, to examine the problem of Being from the perspective of the being who poses the question. The phenomenology discussed in Husserl's diary entry has the same limitation as Jaspers's book: it leaves out the very being who asks the question.

Fundamental ontology asks how matters stand with Being by involving most importantly the one who asks the question, such that the forgetting of Being, alluded to in the passage from Plato's *Sophist* at the beginning of *Sein und Zeit*, can easily be identified with the panoramic objectivity of the phenomenological glance. Looking at the history of Husserl and his student after 1927, we can say that both of them in the year of their falling out were thinking rather vaguely about history, or, as Heidegger would later say, about the history of Being. We must remember that Heidegger, even more than his academic "tutor," was inspired by Dilthey. And it was Dilthey who against Kant had objected that there was no real blood flowing through the veins of the transcendental subject. But this is also just what happens to the transcendental subject, in Kant as in Husserl, who wants to do theory: it becomes an element of the panoramic vision *from nowhere*.

The developments in the thought of the teacher Husserl and his student Heidegger after 1927 say much about what, at least implicitly, was brewing in the debate over fundamental ontology. To pose the problem of the meaning of Being from the point of view of the being asking the question is a step with far-reaching consequences.

For Husserl, the first way is that of grounding the regional ontologies in the transcendental I. But the great unfinished work *The Crisis of the European Sciences*, especially if seen in light of the developments of Heidegger's thought after *Sein und Zeit*, shows that one cannot stop, not even Husserl, at the transcendental I. In order to really be radical, that is, really philosophical, the demand must be to place the I in its historicity under question. While Husserl did not want to go beyond the *Krisis* (of 1936), in his later works Heidegger will speak increasingly often about a "history of Being" that occurs in the concrete historicity of Dasein, of existing human beings. The possibility of authentic (*eigentlich*) existence is given only within the framework of *Ereignis*, of the event of Being. Existential authenticity, therefore, cannot be an individual affair; it involves and it requires a change in the history of Being.[2]

In 1933, as we know, Heidegger joined the Nazi party and gave his famous speech "The Self-Assertion of the German University." We cannot forgive him for that error; however, it did have one of its roots in the need to situate the one who asks the question of Being historically. I will leave aside the debate, which I do not, however, intend to avoid, about why I call Heidegger's Nazi error unpardonable. But even from this development I will rescue this instruction: that the need to abandon realistic metaphysics à la Tarski is motivated not by "theoretical" reasons—which would lead to a new objective or descriptive metaphysics—but by historical needs, what Benjamin called the memory of enslaved forefathers. In the case of Heidegger in the 1910s and 1920s, it is a matter of will, which he shared with the intellectual and artistic avant-garde of that time, and a matter of avoiding the world of "total organization" that was being constructed and therefore appeared as the necessary consequence of positivistic metaphysics. Dilthey, whom I recalled a little while ago, also refers to the famous debate between the human sciences and the natural sciences, which, even on the level of academic philosophy, demonstrated the revolt of the avant-garde against the stratified world that by then was imposing itself everywhere.

There is no contradiction in the rejection of metaphysical "realism" à la Tarski unless one wishes to oppose it with a conception that is more "true." That which inspires the Heideggerian and our rejection of realistic metaphysics is not, to put it briefly, the will of a greater truth—the "discovery" that Tarski's principle is not true—but the need for freedom: the world of metaphysical objectivism that was forming before the eyes of philosophers and artists at the beginning of the last century (remember that Fiat and Ford were born in those same years, and that Frederick Taylor wrote his book *The Principles of Scientific Management* in 1907) rightly appeared to them as a world in which the choices of individual beings would no longer carry any weight.

By looking at the history of Husserl and his student after 1927, we can say that what both were thinking about in the year of their falling out, albeit vaguely, was the history of Being. For Husserl, this path to the history of Being would be realized, in nonetheless unresolved terms, in the *Krisis*, where the preoccupation of carrying eidetic phenomenology back to transcendental subjectivity finds its most authentic sense[3] in the ideal of a restoration of European humanity threatened by the mathematicization of forms of knowledge and by the predominance of the positive sciences in the living world. In Heidegger, as we know, the *Eigentlichkeit* of *Sein und Zeit* was transformed into the idea of Being as *Ereignis*, that is, as the giving (*Gabe, Schicken*) of historico-destinal (*geschichtlich-geschicklich*) openings that constitute the history of Being.

The interest today in rethinking the contentious relationship between Husserl and Heidegger is obviously not only historiographical. To me, it seems that such a rethinking is necessary for two reasons connected to our "attualità" or "present moment," two reasons that are not easily separated. The historical social world in which we live is in many ways only the intensified continuation of that universe of total organization against which the artists and the philosophers of the early-twentieth-century avant-garde were compelled to struggle. Still today it is the world of objectivistic metaphysics against which Heidegger wrote *Sein und Zeit*. Despite the many outbursts of social revolt that we have seen in the decades following the Second World War, the economic and political structures of our society have remained fundamentally the same. The "relapse" of every revolution into authoritarian and bureaucratic routine, the "practico-inert" Sartre discussed in his *Critique of Dialectical Reason*, is right there in front of us. The world of advanced technology, which nonetheless seems to contain many promises for emancipation, grows ever larger by becoming a universe of absolute control over all existence—a control much more strict and intolerable in the very part of the world that we always consider more "developed." Isn't this social world, always substantially more immobile, despite or precisely in virtue of the greatly praised democratic succession, as it was at the beginning of the twentieth century, a product of realistic philosophy, or of metaphysics as Heidegger calls it?

Certainly the realistic philosophies—without placing all of the blame on poor Tarski, of course—provide significant support for the preservation of the status quo: the prize awarded by George Bush to John Searle as a hero of "liberal" American thinking is but one example of this.[4] The very return of phenomenology in recent European culture, which once again takes up the early Husserl, the "eidetic" Husserl, and which is associated with the remains of analytic neoempiricism in order to construct a realistic metaphysics, is a phenomenon of the apologetic acceptance of the existing order. The title of Quine's essay "On What There Is" sounds like a motto shared broadly by the neorealist philosophy that results from a *mésalliance* between evil phenomenologists and evil analytic thinkers.[5] These ontologies have the same objectivistic, panoramic, or simply metaphysical (in the Heideggerian sense of the term) limit, which Heidegger revealed in Jaspers's book and in the eidetic phenomenology of origins: they do not put into play the existence of the philosopher who speaks and formulates the theories. In these ontologies, the Being (of the person, of the various spheres of entities, and so on) can only be unchanging and ahistorical, geometrical like the European science that Husserl declared in crisis. But above all, the lesson that we ought to take from this rethinking of the relation between Husserl and Heidegger is a methodological instruction for philosophy itself: to take note of the oppressive weight of metaphysical realism (here I recall many beautiful pages from Rorty's *Philosophy and the Mirror of Nature*) also means to try to construct a philosophy that is not descriptive—of essences, of nature, of "natural" laws—but projectural.

The philosopher is wrapped up with the very Being about which the question is asked. A sort of principle of indetermination works here: one cannot speak of Being except by participating in it and being an active moment of its history. Interpretation in place of description. A truly "realistic" ontology that does not ignore the fact that it is itself a moment of the Being about which (or in which) it speaks is a hermeneutic ontology. Contrary to the letter of Marx's famous phrase about philosophers who only interpreted the world while trying to change it,[6] it is precisely by interpreting the world—and by not pretending to describe it in its given "objectivity"—that one contributes to its transformation. If all of this means anything, it is clear that we can no longer value a philosophy on the basis of Tarski's principle. What would it mean to say that "there are no facts, only interpretations" is true if and only if there are no facts, and so on? Less than ever can we think that this truth can save us or set us free. The path of thinking followed by the so-called late Heidegger (however, in an Anglo-Saxon environment, let us remember that there is also a "second Wittgenstein," who ended up not too far from him) is completely directed at understanding what it means to think Being not as an objective given, but as the history in which we are involved. And, as with the originary inspiration of *Sein und Zeit*, we are dealing not with a merely theoretical route, but with an out-and-out practico-political itinerary of emancipation.

7

BEING AND EVENT

I n the development of our discussion, through our interpretation
of Heidegger beyond phenomenology, we are bound yet again to
encounter the implications of the conclusion of Nietzsche's sentence: "And this too is an interpretation." Like Heidegger, we want to
exit objectivistic metaphysics because we feel it is a threat to freedom
and the projectuality constitutive of existence. If Being is the objectivity ascertained by rigorous science (what Husserl also thought philosophy ought to be, at least until he declared that the dream was over,
ausgetraeumt), then we living beings do not exist. And it is a matter of
searching for a notion of Being not only that can include us in its theoretical sphere, but more importantly that can in the concreteness of
existence free us from the chains that the society of total organization
places upon us by shaping our life on the idea of the world understood
as objectivity. In the society whose very organization is inspired by the
metaphysics of objectivity, the living being becomes the object itself.

◆ ◆ ◆

It is in the search for a different way of thinking that the idea of the
event matures and that hermeneutic ontology takes shape. I will not
run through the existential analytic from *Sein und Zeit*, where the

grounds for the "*Destruktion* of the history of ontology," or, rather, of objectivistic metaphysics, are put forward. If the search for a different way of thinking Being is motivated, in Heidegger and in us, not so much by theoretical reasons but by the ethical-political will not to accept the world of total organization that metaphysics prepares and accompanies, the existential analysis sheds light on the interpretative nature of every experience and therefore justifies, even on the theoretical level, the intolerance for metaphysics. One cannot even find a good reason in theory for thinking that having an experience of the world means mirroring things objectively. A phenomenological analysis of the world shows that things are not, first and foremost (*zuerst und zumeist*), "objects," but presences that have a significance for us and that can become "objects" of a "pure" description only with a conscious act of abstraction (one also motivated by interest). Things are primarily, in this sense, instruments; and the world is an instrumental totality since an instrument is never given as an isolated thing, but precisely made by something, in view of something else, and so on. We have an experience of things only on the background of this preliminarily given world-totality, which is unveiled to us in the historical language that we find ourselves speaking, and in virtue of which we are always already acquainted with the world. What we call Being, and what we cannot identify with the totality of objects (if not, we do not exist), is rather the horizon in which, as Kant has already taught us to a certain degree, things come to Being. The encounter with things according to an articulation within a horizon of fore-understanding is interpretation. Dilthey had already spoken of interpretation as a knowledge that presupposes some reciprocal belonging between the subject and object (for him it was the case of historical knowledge). Let me explain, especially for those not familiar with Heidegger's text: every verification or falsification of a scientific proposition, of a judgment on an object, is possible only within the paradigms already available to the scientist or the interested scientific community before the individual experiment. Here Thomas Kuhn helps us to go beyond Dilthey: even scientific knowledge is a hermeneutic affair. The horizon of language within which an individual or community experiences the world—namely, within which things come to Being—is historical and finite, Being as one thinks it, or tries to think it. *Sein und Zeit* is a hermeneutic event, a happening of historical-linguistic horizons for which one can speak of a "history of Being."

Allow me to outline very summarily the contents and results of the existential analytic because they are the distant supports of what I propose to call, in the title of this group of lectures, the "end of reality."

The path through which Heidegger constructs these results is not simply the theoretical research that fundamental ontology proposes to "find" and that is "lacking" in Husserlian phenomenology. The urgency of this problem is not in this case motivated by "systematic" reasons. It is moved by practico-political demands, the same that were expressed in the poetry and art of the avant-garde at the beginning of the last century. We should keep in mind its value as an indication of a "philosophical" method that, as I suggested earlier, corresponds to Marx's eleventh thesis on Feuerbach. It also serves as a guiding thread for interpreting the thought of Heidegger (along with every other thinker, moreover) by judging it *iuxta propria principia*, on the basis of its originary motives. That, for example, is also valuable when judging whether the assent to Nazism in 1933 was or was not a gesture "faithful" to these originary motives. If it was not, then there are good arguments for contending that the sympathy for Nazism was not a necessary consequence of Heidegger's philosophy and, indeed, in light of these very motives, can be judged as an error and a self-misunderstanding.

The existential analytic is the basis on which the notion of Being as event develops. Things are as they are given within the thrown project that is revealed in the historical language of a human community. In the language that we speak and that speaks "us" there are always given paradigms within which the world is accessible to us and that we ourselves conceive. In the language that we speak, a collection of criteria for the true and the false is always given, therefore the fact that knowing is the articulation of a fore-understanding does not mean that there is no difference between truth and error, or that *anything goes*.[1] What Heidegger calls the event of Being is not the happening of a successful experiment of "normal science," according to the paradigm in use; it is above all the paradigmatic revolution, the institution of a new historical horizon, the out-and-out birth of a new "world." We can never say a priori what will occur when Being happens—moreover the dialectic of *langue* and *parole* in Sausserian linguistics also testifies to this—and one can also take it as a reference for understanding the ontology (and also the "linguistics") of Heidegger, for which, in this very sense, "language is the house of Being." The event of Being is the happening of truth, in the two senses that the term "truth" has for Heidegger. Truth as *alétheia* is the historical self-giving [*darsi*] of the paradigm, which, by not being the eternal structure of a metaphysical and Parmenidean being, is thought as event. But truth is also the verified proposition according to the very criteria of the paradigm, therefore normal science in Kuhn's sense. If the essay "The Origin of the Work of Art" (1936) says that the work is "truth setting itself to work," the meaning of the term "truth" must be understood in the first sense: the work of art is the foundation of a world, the experience that we have of it; according to Heidegger, it changes the coordinates within which the world appears to us. It is obvious that this emphatic significance of aesthetic experience counts for those great "epochal" works that Heidegger has in mind: Homer's poems for the Greek world, the Bible for all of Western culture, perhaps Dante, Shakespeare, Hölderlin. But Joyce's *Ulysses*? Or even a small sonata by Vivaldi? Here too, it is difficult to establish— as in the aforementioned case of *langue* and *parole*—where to find the limit between "normal" and "revolutionary." Certainly in the case of art, since we are not talking about the production of objects of use that clearly remain within the paradigm, we must always say that some "revolution" happens: the reading of a Dostoyevsky novel really changes our view of the world, therefore it really opens a new paradigm for the one who has the experience—nothing is as it was before.

The historico-linguistic horizons in which for Heidegger the Kantian a priori is dissolved must be thought as events.[2] Even if we never see the "birth" of a new world, we can only think Being in this way if we do not want to fall back into the objectivistic metaphysics that renders our existential historicity unthinkable. In the essay on the work of art from 1936, Heidegger also alludes to other ways that truth happens, beyond the work of art: a new world can also be born from a great moral or intellectual experience, or from the foundation of a political order. These indications remain obscure because in the works that follow, Heidegger will continue to seek out the happening of truth only in poetry and in the great words of the origins (Hölderlin, Anaximander, Rilke, and so on). It seems clear why he did not develop the discourse on politics: he has just returned from the misadventure with Nazism and he preferred to not occupy himself with political events. Concentrating on the event of truth that happens in art also allowed him to construct an idealized image of the event of Being, which seems to set aside every conflictual element. The essay on the work of art also spoke of a "conflict" between "world" and "earth" that characterizes the work. The conflict (Heidegger uses the term *Streit*, "conflict," and *Riss*, "rift")[3] was intended in various ways and merits greater discussion. What interests us here, however, is the very notion of conflict, which both the aesthetics inspired by Heidegger and the philosophical hermeneutics that began with him (I am thinking above all about my teacher Gadamer) have interpreted in a very "peaceful" way. As we know, Gadamer constructed his hermeneutics around the theme of dialogue; truth, we can say by taking up his thought, is event as it is the "fusion of horizons" (*Horizontverschmelzung*) that is verified as the always provisional conclusion of a dialogue between diverse positions. The pragmatic definition of truth that we also find in Rorty (the true is that which is good for us) easily leads back to this idea of agreement. And obviously Habermas's theory of communicative action is also part of this general dialogical atmosphere.[4] The popularity of hermeneutics is still today largely based on the reputation of the philosophy of dialogue, to which every debate has by now returned—on the relation between parties within a nation, on the relation between diverse cultures in a multiethnic society, on the peace between social classes or in the Middle East.

Perhaps this excessive popularity has made hermeneutics a commonplace. Yet again, as during the time of the existentialist Heidegger early in the twentieth century, what calls our (my, at least) attention to the conflict that is inseparable from the happening of truth is not the demand for a theoretical clarification, but the need to react to an "external" situation, or, better, a condition of culture in which it seems even philosophy finds itself. The new "realism" that, according to me, characterizes the atmosphere of both continental and postanalytic philosophy today could be characterized with the Heideggerian term "lack of emergency" [*Notlosigkeit*].5 The importance in our view given to the notion of event also seems to me conditioned by the situation in which we live, and in which nothing seems to happen. Certainly newspapers and other forms of information are full of "events," and yet the dominant impression of the citizens of the industrialized world, whether at its center or on the periphery and in the postcolonial slums, is that nothing ever happens anymore. The participation of citizens in the democratic elections of many countries, especially in Europe, continues to decline; and it would be difficult to argue that people avoid the polls because they are doing well and they do not need any change. The fact is that a general resignation dominates, one that remains undisturbed even when there is an economic crisis like the one that we are experiencing now.

What makes us speak against the lack of emergency, or, better, what makes us feel this lack, this want, is the same discomfort that inspired Heidegger at the time of *Sein und Zeit*: lack of emergency means lack of liberty, the identification of Being with the present order of entities and of thought as the mirroring of the world as it is. We are again faced with the originary motives that inspired Heidegger, and that are the necessary roots of any philosophy. The philosopher doesn't just respond to theoretical questions by searching to complete a system—for example, phenomenology—with what it is lacking (in the case of Husserl it was fundamental ontology), or by resolving the problems opened up by a theory. I pointed to the profound ethical need that moved Husserl and that pushed him to search for a fundamental ontology. In Heidegger, who was much more religiously motivated than the "mathematical" Husserl, the will to do philosophy as a search for existential authenticity is yet more profound and irreducible to any "professional" motivation (to this idea, remember that Husserl also spoke of the philosopher as a "professional of the human condition").[6]

In conclusion, how does the coming to light of a "notion" of Being as hermeneutic event respond to the originary motivations of Heideggerian inquiry? We know that this idea of philosophy as a path to emancipation is as old as philosophy itself. What is the task of philosophy in a theory that no longer conceives of Being in metaphysical terms, as the given that the mind must only try to mirror in the most faithful and adequate way? "Knowing" that Being is not an object but an event does not set us free. The Heideggerian effort to exit from metaphysics is motivated by the need to overcome the forgetting of Being in favor of entities and their givenness, which is precisely what dominates metaphysics. But once again, what does it mean to "remember Being," to exit from forgetting? What I have tried really hard to show is that remembering Being means thinking it radically as event—as a happening that we do not observe from a neutral vantage point, but in which we participate actively as interpreters. As participating interpreters we cannot but live the event in terms of conflict. The truth sets us free and redeems us—with this I return to my point of departure—only insofar as we participate actively in its event by committing ourselves to the conflict. I already recalled that the human, according to one of the more grandiloquent images of Heidegger, is the "shepherd of Being." He is not the lord of it, but in many ways he is responsible for it. If he does not decisively assume his own responsibility, that of making truth happen at the expense of conflict, it is Being itself that gets lost in the metaphysical forgetting.

Truth, namely, the new world that is instituted, as one sees in art when new paradigms are opened, does not happen through a natural process as occurs with growth. Certainly, Heidegger seems at times to think that death is "the casket of Being" because the succession of generations is also the condition for the renewal of worldviews, namely, for the happening of truth. But the event of truth not only reflects the natural succession of generations. This succession is also and above all conflict: between the generations themselves, at times, but in general between interpretations that are mutually exclusive, and that differ from one another not only as diverse artistic "styles" in an ideal museum where the peace of "aesthetic" values reigns. More importantly, we are dealing with the great historical struggles, with social systems that want to take the place of others, in the name of that which, in the terminology of the essay on the work of art, we could call "earth": the needs of survival, the common ties pre- or ir-rational, the will to free oneself from intolerable servitude, beginning with poverty.

The absence of emergency is perhaps the most complete form of the forgetting of Being that belongs to metaphysics. That today nothing might happen seems difficult to believe. And yet even the big crises that we have lived through and that we continue to live through do not give rise to a "paradigmatic" novelty in the sociopolitical sense. September 11? It only gave the United States more reasons to intensify its various forms of control, but it did not give the country reasons for any transformation of "regime." The same goes in the global economy: it is true that there are new protagonists—China, India, Brazil—but their "emergence" is only a chance to run for the position of the current rulers (China especially "emerges" because it is developing into a large capitalistic country). And could you imagine a "conversion" in our world? Religions have also become ever more dialogical, ever more generic: true, there are fundamentalists, but even the extreme tone of the preaching of certain religious exponents is a sign that, for precisely this reason, the perceived risk is the loss of a truly alternative identity. There is a term that I use from Carl Schmitt—without committing myself to a philologically faithful rendering of it: *Neutralisierung*, that sort of leveling of differences in which our democracies are masters (certainly Schmitt did not like this, but should that to be pleasing to us?), where *plus ça change plus c'est la même chose*. Even the "revolutionary" importance that experimental science had in modernity is by now consumed in the game of foundations, of military funding, in the increasingly tight connection between research and economic and political powers (with the prevalence of the first). Is there anyone left who on ethical-political topics thinks to place one's trust in the opinion of "esteemed scientists," of Nobel Prize winners (yes, the prize funded by dynamite)? The "globalization" of the economy from which thinkers and democratic politicians expect so much has ended up producing an intensification of control. The differences between the rich—ever less numerous—and the poor, always increasing in number and in poverty, have grown exponentially in those very years of the globalized economy. And those who possess power in this world, from the authority of individual countries to those of the great supranational unions (now there is even the European Union, another hope that we continue to cultivate with ever weakening conviction, and also NATO, a sort of gross international police in service of the United States), preach above all the value of stability; even the recurring crises are not approached as occasions for transformation, but as temporary difficulties to be resolved with successive restorations of order quo ante.

What does all of this have to do with the destiny of Being, with the claim to take leave of the forgetting into which the long domination of metaphysics (as well as the metaphysics of domination) has fallen deeply? Again and again we find ourselves with the notion of event: if Being cannot think itself as the unchanging givenness of the object (which would remove every sense of freedom and novelty from existence), then it can be nothing other than event. But there where nothing (more) happens or can happen, of Being as such nothing more remains, according to the Nietzschean definition of nihilism. That for us, and for (our) Heidegger, means that, with the absence of the event, namely, of Being, there would no longer be "difference"—the existing order would be the only one and would be definitively true and there would no longer be an alternative horizon to oppose to it. Are we professing vitalism? We do not know if it is a metaphysical thesis ("there is" only life and its renewal). For our present, this means with all our strength standing against those who reject difference, conflict, change—against those who forget and want to make us forget Being itself.

8

THE ETHICAL DISSOLUTION
OF REALITY

A	t this point it seems particularly difficult to pass from the con-
clusions of my previous lecture, about truth as event always
characterized by conflict, to that which I announced with the
title, "The Ethical Dissolution of Reality." It is a difficulty to which I
have already alluded by remembering, first, that hermeneutics is always
seen primarily as the philosophy of dialogue and therefore appears as
a conciliatory thinking. I also said that this "irenic" reading is responsible, or perhaps the effect, of a certain banalization that hermeneutics
has endured by becoming a sort of *koiné*, a shared background of our
culture, and not just of philosophy. It appears obvious to everyone,
above all in democracy, that dialogue is preferred over conflict. When
I think about this blatant misunderstanding of the sense of hermeneutics, I am reminded of a passage from Nietzsche's *Thus Spoke Zarathustra*, where Zarathustra, by recounting the vision from his dream
of a shepherd who was choking on a snake that had entered his throat,
announces his doctrine of the eternal return of the same—by interpreting the snake as a symbol of the circle of time that always returns. The
animals that, in the literary fiction, accompany Zarathustra immediately interpret the parable as a joyful announcement: "everything goes,
everything comes back, eternally rolls the wheel of Being." And Zarathustra rebukes them because they have turned the doctrine of return

into "a hurdy-gurdy song." They must not forget that the snake is going to choke the shepherd from the dream unless he bites its head off. And that's it: hermeneutics understood as the doctrine of "dialogical" conciliation, stripped of the severity of dialectic, namely, of conflict, is reduced to a hurdy-gurdy song.

◆ ◆ ◆

The idea that hermeneutics is a theory of the dialogical conciliation of historical conflicts was also helped by its formulation as "weak thought," which I defended in recent, primarily Continental, philosophy along with a group of Italian colleagues (especially Pier Aldo Rovatti, the disciple of Enzo Paci and thus of a phenomenological upbringing). The idea of weakness, as the readers of my works know, is the result of a sort of "contamination" (in the Latin sense, *contaminatio*, "mixing") between the nihilism of Nietzsche and the ontology of Heidegger. The famous title of a section of Nietzsche's *Twilight of the Idols*—"Wie die 'wahre Welt' endlich zur Fabel wurde" ("How the 'true world' became a fable")—sums up the unfolding of Western philosophy as the progressive development of nihilism. It is the same process that Heidegger calls the end of metaphysics, that history through which, in the end, "there is nothing left of Being as such."[1] Now, as we know, the always open problem of Heidegger interpretation is whether or not he has overcome nihilism. The interpretation I have proposed, under the name of "weak thought," is founded on the idea that Nietzsche and Heidegger must be read "together." (I also wrote, years ago, an essay titled "Nietzsche, Heidegger's Interpreter.")[2] The ontology of Heidegger is not a "recovery" of Being beyond nihilism, as he himself often seemed to think. Being can only be remembered (*Denken-Andenken*) as passed. If one wished to discuss it, it would also be possible to show that Heidegger's Nazi error in 1933 consisted in the very belief that a nonmetaphysical "recovery" of Being was possible, which according to him must take place in Nazi

Germany as antimodern, anticapitalist, and able to return to a type of pre-Socratic civilization. The idea that Being could "return" seems to me a profound contradiction with respect to what Heidegger called "ontological difference," according to which Being never gives itself as present, because it would thus become an entity, even the supreme entity, "given" like the others. There would be a multitude of consequences from such a return: for example, there would be authoritarianism and certainly violence; questions would no longer be possible in front of Being itself given in presence; there would not even be any "history" or any freedom.

The no-longer-metaphysical Being that Heidegger tries to think can therefore only be the "consumed" Being that appears in Nietzsche's nihilism. One of the best-known aspects of nihilism is what Nietzsche calls "the transvaluation of the highest values." Now, Being thought as event and not as eternal foundation outside of time and history realizes just this aspect of nihilism: "antifoundationalism" is the term that a thinker like Richard Rorty, for example, has taught us to designate this condition of thinking. As far as he is concerned, in order not to be presented as a metaphysical-objective description of the absence of foundations, "weak thought" furthermore adds that the transvaluation and absence of foundation must be thought as a historical process in which we ourselves are involved. "There is" no absence of foundation; a "transvaluation" happens, and Nietzsche also uses this term to allude to a process and not to a stable given. Thus, Heidegger cannot say that Being is not foundation, but *is* event. There is no event; rather, an event happens. And since it is the event of Being, we are always involved, even we who speak about it.

Being, for weak thought that remains faithful to Heidegger, is the event of the ontological difference in action: Being gives itself as the distancing from entities understood as objective givenness. The return of Being, the remembering of it to which Heidegger invited us, consists in the progressive weakening of what is given as stable, value, principle, unavoidable given.

Here we must remember the title of a great book on Heidegger by Reiner Schürmann—*Heidegger on Being and Acting: From Principles to Anarchy*—a colleague who died too young some years ago after having taught many years at the New School for Social Research in New York. Apart from the literal meaning of the term "anarchy," Heidegger's thought—understood as "weak thought"—appears as a theory that claims it must refute all absolutes, whether theoretical (metaphysical evidence claims, first principles) or practical (the natural foundation of laws, or also the foundation of politics on science, especially on political economy).

Yet this is a nonviolent anarchy. After all, Nietzsche, who also spoke often of the will to power, never intended it as a philosophy of struggle and of physical violence; this type of violence also assumes material supremacy as an absolute that must triumph at any cost. Weak thought considers the "transvaluation of the highest values" also and above all as a promotion of nonviolent human relations; violence appears to him only as the silencing of the other, or the silencing of every question apart from absolute and unquestionable first principles. Violence always acts on the basis of absolute affirmations, whether in the many forms of private violence it takes its own desire, advantage, or preference as absolute, or whether a historical authority can justify much greater violence in the name of claimed absolute values.

Weak thought, as hermeneutic thinking, is certainly a thinking of dialogue that is established on the very disappearance of absolutes, by really taking itself as the inheritor of the Christian ideal of charity. If the Christian churches have often persecuted heretics and unbelievers in the name of truth clearly understood as absolute (*amicus Plato, sed magis amica veritas*), weak thought holds that precisely because absolute truth is "liquidated," transvalued like all of the highest values, one can finally practice charity, the Christian love of one's fellow human. Absolute truth is therefore exchanged for the agreement with others reached through the process of negotiation, whether in the private sphere or in the field of politics. And, as for Christianity, Jesus Christ is here thought as the living sign that God himself wanted to free himself from his absolute nature by becoming like us.

But why an "ethical dissolution of reality"? Everything depends on a radical reading of the page in *Sein und Zeit* to which I have already referred: there is Being, not entities, insofar as there is truth. And it is very likely that this radical sense might not have been Heidegger's intention when he wrote these words. But he ought to have and could be understood in that way; or at least, given the path that Heidegger followed after *Sein und Zeit*, this meaning of the text, which I would call normative, seems to be the most plausible and coherent. If there is an "end" at which to aim for whoever wishes to take leave of the metaphysics of the given, of Being as supreme objective entity, the end would be neither a final reconciliation in the One nor something like the contemplation of the light that reveals it. What we "know" of Being is that it makes itself known to the degree that it goes beyond, and leaves aside, beings. The normative sense that we read in Heidegger's passage is not, moreover, a metaphysical sense—it does not describe a hierarchy between Being and entities. As with a text of the Gospels, we would say that it is written "only for our instruction," namely, it has only an ethical sense, appeals to our freedom, that is, to our *An-denken* of Being. To reduce violence and the supremacy of entities that pretend to be true Being (for example, as one sees with nonnegotiable principles that today are increasingly utilized by fundamentalists) and all of the violence that is legitimated in the name of the absolutized entity (Stephen Dedalus, again, home, country, church) is the road to the dissolution of the reality that corresponds to the nihilistic vocation of Being. It is and can only be an ethical dissolution—therefore a "duty" that one never completes and that above all is not realized in a theoretical rejection of the "real world," as the critics of hermeneutics had once thought. Moreover, even the call to remember Being does not have a content that "fulfills" it, in which one might find peace by reaching a certain condition. The only sense of the call is that which in the Gospels invites the faithful to be suspicious of whoever is revealed to be the Messiah returned to the world. It is an ethical-political program that certainly appears weak because it does not have absolute values as a point of reference; and yet, it is a program that is not in any way easy or reassuring.

APPENDIX IV

METAPHYSICS AND VIOLENCE

A Question of Method

I f contemporary philosophy wants to continue its work as philosophy, that is, if it wants to be something more than merely essay writing or the historiography of the thought that has come before it and to avoid being reduced to a purely auxiliary discipline of the positive sciences (as epistemology, methodology, or logic), it must recognize a preliminary problem that is posed by the radical critique of metaphysics. The adjective "radical" is emphasized because only this sort of critique of metaphysics truly constitutes an unavoidable preliminary problem for every philosophical discourse aware of its responsibility. Those forms of the critique of metaphysics that, more or less explicitly, restrict themselves to considering it just one philosophical point of view among others—a school or current in thinking that for some philosophically argued reason one ought to abandon today—should not be considered radical. For example, the widespread scientism of twentieth-century thought takes it as more or less evident that one must no longer do metaphysics but rather epistemology, method, logic, or even just the analysis of language. This total "transfer of duties" from traditional philosophy to a scientistic philosophy that can no longer distinguish itself from science (whether as purely auxiliary thought or as the positive scientific approach to everything belonging to a particular domain of philosophy, namely, the human sciences) can be contrasted with a defense of metaphysics as the "science of spirit," as the place where one elaborates those self-descriptions in which conscience may achieve the elaboration of its own fundamental conflicts (Dieter Henrich), in which it may achieve what is ultimately a renewed theory of self-knowledge, such as the one clearly defined by Kant as particular to modern metaphysics.[1] This "transfer of duties" not only brings with it the reconsideration of the metaphysics of self-knowledge as its unavoidable shadow and correlate, but also carries an obvious metaphysical residue that remains unconsumed to the degree that, as seen in positivism, it simply transfers the locus of truth from traditional metaphysics to the natural or human sciences, or that it simply recovers metaphysics as "semantic-linguistic" ontology in the sense exemplified by Donald Davidson.[2] Even in this case the critique of metaphysics, classically understood, does not become radical because—as happens in many areas of neoempirical thought, even within a Popperian idea of metaphysics—its detachment from the metaphysics of the past nonetheless occurs through an explicit terminological continuity that may even express a conceptual continuity. In question here is a philosophical theory of the most general and "constitutive" features of the world of experience, even if they are not thought linguistically but objectively. The observations regarding the limited radicality of the critique of positivistic metaphysics can even be extended to the various forms of "reductionist naturalism" (as Dieter Henrich has called it, using a Nietzschean expression),[3] to the various "schools of suspicion." These schools consider metaphysical propositions, all of the "primary self-interpretations" of humanity and of Being (once again, Henrich's expression), as fictions that are brought back and dissolve in reference to the explication of the conditions that determined their formation. Even in these reductionist positions, one has to judge to what degree the suspicion has the courage to be truly radical. The most recent developments of one of the most self-revealing and articulated "reductionist naturalisms" of the last century, Marxism, can also be interpreted as the radicalization of suspicion and the liquidation of every metaphysical residue—that is, at least as regards "Western" Marxism, even in its political manifestations, including the recent crisis and dissolution of communist parties.

The critique of metaphysics is radical and it presents itself as an unavoidable preliminary problem, a real "question of method," not only where its formation touches upon determinate ways of doing philosophy or its determinate subject matter, but where it treats the very possibility of philosophy as such, that is, as the discourse characterized by its logical and even, inseparably, its social constitution.

Nietzsche is the master of this radical critique of metaphysics. According to him, philosophy formed and developed as the search for a "true world" that would be able to provide a reassuring foundation in place of the uncertain mutability of the visible world. This true world has been, over time, identified with the Platonic Ideas, the Christian afterlife, the Kantian a priori, and the positivist's unknowable. The logic that was the force behind all of these transformations—the need to seek out a true world that was authentically so, one able to withstand critique and "provide a foundation"—eventually led him to recognize the very idea of truth as a fable, a useful fiction in determinate conditions of experience. Such conditions have disappeared, a fact expressed by the discovery of truth as a fiction. The problem that Nietzsche seems to open at this point, in a world where even the unmasking attitude is unmasked, is one of nihilism. Once its nature is discovered to be produced and "functional" rather than originary, do we really have to think that the destiny of thought and of the very belief in the value of truth or foundation is to establish itself without illusions, as an *esprit fort* in the world of the war of all against all, where the "weak perish" and only power is affirmed? Or will it rather be the case, as Nietzsche hypothesizes at the end of the long fragment on "European Nihilism" (from summer 1887), that in this environment those who are destined to triumph are the "most moderate, those who have no *need* of extreme articles of faith, those who not only admit, but also love a good deal of contingency and nonsense"?

Nietzsche does not really develop this allusion to the "most moderate," but it is likely that, as his notes from his final years indicate (the same notes that produce this fragment on nihilism), the most moderate one is the artist, the one who knows how to experiment with a freedom derived, without doubt, from having overcome even the interest in survival.[4] It is clear that in this sense his critique of metaphysics is radical: if we accept it, we can no longer continue to philosophize in a world where even philosophy is nothing more than a struggle, a play of forces, the conflict of interpretations. And yet, to the degree that it appears unmasked, it cannot truly be a conflict. Nietzsche does not develop an alternative to the supremacy of the most moderate, nor does his critique result in something "nonphilosophical" or, rather problematically, artistic, as Nietzsche senses the unsustainability of yet another "metaphysical" solution. Such would be the case if moderateness were identified with a transcendental description, a sort of historicism à la Dilthey, which would make philosophy coincide with a systematic description of the Weltanschauungen in conflict. This would posit a true world once again, that of the sovereign, historical consciousness, an extreme rediscovery of the Socratic wisdom that confidently claims to know that it does not know.

The link between metaphysics and violence is a less aporetic trait, perhaps one more characteristic of the discourse Nietzsche has with metaphysics, one that provides an unavoidable stage for current philosophy. This connection is presented not univocally but rather in a multiform way that is suggestive precisely in its irreducibility to a definite schema. This connection has two features: on the one side, the unmasking of the metaphysics that marks the advent of nihilism reveals its ties to a condition of violence and is an act of violence itself. As the thinking of foundation, the illusions of grasping the heart of reality, the first principle on which "everything" depends, it was "an effort to take possession, by an act of strength, of the most fruitful lands,"[5] an effort that, through a sort of magical reassurance, was reacting to an extremely insecure condition of existence, namely, the condition of humanity before the birth of rationalization and domestication made possible by the very discipline put forward in the name of the metaphysical fictions. Today these fictions are no longer required. The individual of rationalized society no longer needs these extreme forms of reassurance; one can live in "proximity," modeling his own thoughts on science—not because it is true, objective knowledge, but because it is a form of thinking less bothered by the problem of salvation and individual destiny: "'What do I matter!'—stands over the door of the thinker of the future."[6] This is the relatively "optimistic" Nietzsche of the "philosophy of morning" that is ultimately put forth in *Human, All Too Human* and constitutes the fundamental intonation of those works that appear in the Enlightenment period of Nietzsche's work, from *Human, All Too Human* to *Daybreak* to *The Gay Science*. The later writings (following, however, indications that are already present, for example, in *The Gay Science*), such as the fragment on nihilism just mentioned, insist on a second, inseparable aspect of the crisis of metaphysics, a crisis that occurs in relation to a manifesting of violence as such. This could occur in the more evident sense that once metaphysical beliefs are weakened, there is no longer anything that limits the conflictual nature of existence, the struggle between weak and strong for a supremacy no longer legitimated by anything (*Grund*, natural or divine laws, and so on), but by the mere fact of imposing itself; or it could occur in the sense that seems decisive for Nietzsche (and for the problem of metaphysics in general), whereby the weakening of metaphysical beliefs not only uncovers the violence of existence for what it is and makes it no longer possible, but is born already as the result of an outburst of violence.[7]

It is difficult to say if the philosophical theses of the late Nietzsche—such as the idea of the eternal return, the *Übermensch*, the will to power—do or do not represent a solution to the problem of placing these two aspects of the critique of metaphysics together. Would the unmasking of the violence have any meaning if it only led to further violence, even if it were unmasked? At stake is more than just the repugnance that comes with accepting that the result of Nietzsche's philosophy is the apology for a return to a primitive, wild state; what also matters is the intimate contradictory nature of the thesis: the Nietzschean conception of the "symbolic forms," namely, of ideological productions, of the metaphysical, moral, religious fictions, seems to exclude the fact that they act only as superfluous maskings. Considering the problem in this way would still mean professing the typically metaphysical belief in the "naked" truth of the thing itself. The unmasked truth would be "better" only insofar as it ends up being "more true." In some way, therefore, the two features of the link between metaphysics and violence must be of value together. The radical critique of metaphysics does its work to the very degree that it seeks, and eventually finds, a "thinkable" conjunction between the two by resolving the question of their relation more clearly than Nietzsche does, and yet still on the path that he opens. In fact, it is likely that the Nietzsche renaissance characteristic of European thought since the beginning of the 1960s is motivated by the very clarity of his presentation of the problem of metaphysics's end and its relation to the question of violence, rather than by the rediscovery of the "constructive" theses of Nietzsche, which still remain problematic. With this "discovery," a decisive intuition, and the opening of a discourse, Nietzsche anticipates the complex meaning of many, if not all, discourses that are at the center of philosophical attention from the end of the nineteenth century to today. With Nietzsche we can consider the impossibility of the continuation of metaphysics in relation to the unmasking of violence; but one should remember that the features indicated above (the theoretical unmasking of the school of suspicion and the practical-political coming to light of a violence without limits) are meant to summarize—in one point that becomes the undeniable beginning of twentieth-century philosophy and the "question of method" from which one must begin—the transformations and crises that philosophy has undergone in the last one hundred years.

This affirmation is very risky given the "apocalyptic" tone that seems to characterize it, and it can be consummated only through its further elaboration (which leads it to a conclusion opposed to any apocalyptic temptation). Its verisimilitude seems tied to the preliminary decision to privilege a certain line of twentieth-century thought—primarily that which stands between existentialism, phenomenology, and Hegelian-Marxist critical theory—over those more "sober" currents, even more professional, that first and foremost developed the critique of knowledge. Two observations must be put forward here: one is "historical," and the other is systematic. From the point of view of the interpretation of the history of twentieth-century philosophy, one can with verisimilitude maintain that to emphasize the connection between metaphysics and violence in the various forms in which it appears in Nietzsche is not to mistake what at first glance seems the problem universally considered as central—that of the relation between philosophy and science. Neither the problematic of the distinction between the natural and the human sciences nor the problematic that is developed within the epistemology of the sciences of nature (from the dispute over the foundations of mathematics to neopositivist physicalism to the later developments of analytic philosophy) could be described solely as responses to the theoretical demand to reestablish the relations between these forms of knowledge according to the affirmation of the importance of the experimental science of nature—taken more and more generally as the model for every form of knowledge that wants to be socially more definitive and effective. It is the more or less explicit reference to the rationalization of society as the event that reveals the connection between metaphysics and violence that determines the central meaning of the epistemology of the human sciences in their relation to the natural sciences in today's philosophical debate. These terms were often left unspoken until the Nietzsche renaissance brought them forth. The connection between phenomenology and existentialism, on the one hand, and expressionism and avant-gardism, on the other, was already thoroughly explored and is by now somewhat commonplace. It must be clarified, however, that even Dilthey and the seemingly exclusively epistemological problematic of the foundation of the human sciences belong to this same climate (within which one could also include Bergson in France, Croce in Italy, and, a bit later, Bloch and the first members of the Frankfurt School and, obviously, the existentialists, Heidegger most of all), which finds literary and, more broadly, cultural expression in the avant-garde and which appeals to the irreducibility of the "spiritual" in the face of scientific-technological rationality, which, according to the theoretical dream of the positivists, has become a social reality.

Neither the theoretical problem of scientific knowledge's refoundation nor even the demand to make the human sciences more rigorous serves as a motive for the Heidegger of *Being and Time* or even for the Husserl of the *Krisis*. They, in diverse yet profoundly connected forms, reflect philosophically on the distaste for the rationalization of existence guided by the mathematical sciences of nature. Heidegger reproposes the problem of Being in *Being and Time* because the concept of Being transmitted by European metaphysics merely thinks the Being of the object of the positive sciences: the verified, measured, manipulated object of science and technology that derives from it can exhaustively describe what is and are completely unfolded as present in front of us, with neither past nor future, something other than the not-yet-present and the no-longer-present. This concept of Being "does not work" and requires a revision by Heidegger not because it is not theoretically adequate: rather, it is in reality an attack on existence (as Kierkegaard already thought of Hegel's metaphysical rationalism). Not only does it make it impossible for one to think conceptually about one's own lived experience, so intimately permeated with projection toward the future and with memories of the past, but, above all, it is one with the practical, social undertaking of the rationalization of society and existence in terms of "total organization."

The "reduction" to the unmasking of violence, proposed by Nietzsche through the problem of the impossibility of the continuation of metaphysics, appears harder to accept if one looks at the epistemological, logical, and methodological problematic associated with positivistic philosophy. Yet, even in this landscape, it appears with increasing clarity that their dominant concerns were not exclusively theoretical or epistemological, or, at least, that they enter into a picture of culture that is also marked by the themes of the avant-garde. Such an awareness—one that matures through historiographical self-knowledge, beginning with the discovery of "Wittgenstein's Vienna"[8]—is surely not theoretically enough to justify the Nietzschean "reduction," even in the face of the "epistemological" line of twentieth-century thought. It nevertheless seems justifiable to maintain that even the purely *erkenntnistheoretisch* themes of analytic philosophy reveal their profound connections with the "Nietzschean" theme of the relation between metaphysics, scientific rationality, and violence. This revelation may occur on the basis of renewed historiographical self-knowledge that came along with "Wittgenstein's Vienna" or on the basis of the centrality assumed in recent years in the philosophical-analytic realm by the debate about themes like Kuhn's paradigms or about the epistemological anarchism of Feyerabend and Lakatos (themes in which one finds an ever-growing awareness of the relation between the verification or falsification of propositions and the historical-social existence of the scientific community, in which, as a matter of fact, every validity "counts"), including all of the historical, political, and economic implications that come with them. Or it may occur on the basis of the increasingly fragmented anthropological interpretation or "application" of the Wittgensteinian theory of language-games and of their relations (the relation between diverse language-games, their ultimate incommensurability, the possibility of a metagame or nevertheless of a procedure of translation are increasingly tied to the question of the relation between diverse cultural universes, for example, different civilizations, colonizers and colonized, and so on). The reasons for the exposure of this connection are more than merely contingent (for example, it is certain that a decisive factor for American thought was the Vietnam War, and as proof one could cite a certain diminished openness to these themes in British thought), but one can appeal to a continuity both in the "anthropological" thread of classical positivism and in its usefulness for science, in view of the rationalization and humanization of social relations.

These arguments, and other similar ones more historiographically articulated, can be advanced on the historical level in order to legitimate the Nietzschean reduction of the problem of metaphysics to the problem of violence, which is proposed here as the initial point of attack for every philosophical discourse today. But there is also a systematic observation that produces a more coherent outcome. The question that deals with the end of metaphysics and the impossibility of its continuation is an urgent one not just or principally because, as I think, it appears to be the explicit or implicit motive for the main currents of twentieth-century philosophy, but, above all, because it engages the very possibility of continuing to philosophize. Now, this possibility is not really threatened by the discovery of other methods, other types of discourse, other sources of truth that, if sought out, would be able to do without philosophizing and metaphysical arguing. The unmasked connection that these procedures of foundation entertain with domination and violence shines the light of suspicion on philosophy as such and on every discourse that wants once again to engage, on different levels and through different methods, in the procedures of "foundation" and the affirmation of originary structures, principles, and coherent evidence. The reference to this connection, even if it seems accidental, is rather one that, taken seriously, makes the critique of metaphysics truly radical. Without it, every metaphysical truth claim is simply replaced with other "truths" that, without a critical or radical dissolution of the very notion of truth, wind up proposing new foundational events. As one might be tempted to do by referring back to Hegel, this "question of method" could be contrasted with the act of jumping into water in order to learn how to swim. That is, one could construct philosophical arguments by seeing if it is not possible, against every exaggerated suspicion, to identify some certainties that are somehow "ultimate" and generally shared. Nevertheless, the invitation to throw oneself into the water, the invitation to philosophize, does not arrive from nowhere. It necessarily recalls us to the existence of a tradition, of a language, of a method. The inheritances that we receive from this tradition, however, are not all the same. Among them there is the Nietzschean announcement of the death of God, which is an "experience" more than a theory—the end of metaphysics and, with it, the end of philosophy. If one wants to accept the responsibility that the inheritance of the philosophy of the past places upon us, one cannot dismiss the preliminary question of this "experience." This very faith in philosophy compels us first of all not to avoid the question of its radical negation, a question that, as we have seen, is inextricably linked to the question of violence.

Two masters of recent thought pose the problem of metaphysics in these terms—Theodor Adorno and Emmanuel Lévinas. Perhaps their lesson is the only one that really "jumps headlong" into the Nietzschean themes widespread in all of contemporary culture—the unavoidable question that ties the destiny of metaphysics to the destiny of violence. And yet, with respect to Nietzsche and above all to Heidegger, the shared goals of their thinking seem to configure solutions that still remain within the framework of metaphysical thinking.

Adorno's "negative dialectic," as we know, connects the crisis of metaphysics, the impossibility of its continuation, to its tragic parody represented by Auschwitz, but also, more broadly, by the world of total administration. The contempt that metaphysics shows for the transient, the body, the individual in its specific and accidental singularity objectively "prepares" for the extermination of great masses of humans in the name of a theory or even for their subservience to the global rationalization of existence, as one finds in the totally administered society of the advanced technological world. This occurs beyond the intentions of any philosophers or their culture. In Adorno, what happens to metaphysics is something that happens more specifically to the truth of the Hegelian system: while Hegel's thesis that truth is the whole was a valid one for him, today when this truth is realized in the administered world as a parody, the whole becomes the false. Through its "realization," in some way metaphysics is revealed as the thinking of violence (according to a thesis that we have already discovered in Nietzsche). But the right that sanctions the revolt of offended transience, individuality, and existence against the violence of extermination and total administration is nonetheless one of transcendental metaphysics, the *promesse de bonheur* that legitimates every critical and ethical distancing from the state of present affairs. Metaphysical violence is not just any return from transience to the other, and not just any passage from "here to there," from appearance to truth, from the accidental to the essential. What belies metaphysics is its unfolding in presence as a totalizing realization: a thesis particularly close to Heidegger's, by which metaphysics ends when it culminates in the actual techno-scientific rationalization of the world, which removes every transcendence and turns it into totally immanent presence. Unlike Heidegger, however, Adorno seems to claim that we can separate metaphysics as the *promesse de bonheur*, as a utopian reference to an authenticity transcending the present state of affairs, from its unfolding in totalizing rationality and in violence. That equates to "seizing and revoking the movement of false reconciliation,"[9] what has realized the absolute nature of Hegelian spirit in the form of a parody. This reduces the *promesse de bonheur* to appearance—the appearance that also characterizes the beautiful in Kant's *Critique of Judgment*—and to the *presque rien*. The happiness that constitutes the content of the metaphysical promise, that to which the finite, in its ephemeral and accidental nature, rightfully aspires, is the dialectical reconciliation that is also the telos of Hegel's absolute spirit: a fully unfolded self-knowledge no longer at odds with nature and therefore, in some way, no longer finite. In respect to this ideal of a reconciled subject—one that is transferred to a utopian horizon by Adorno and counts as the unique and only "true" norm of emancipation—the "revocation" of the movement of sublation, the return of the Kantian appearance and the revelation of metaphysical transcendence in the *presque rien*, has nothing other than the flavor of a pure and simple relapse. In effect, the "conclusive" position taken by *Aesthetic Theory* in Adorno's philosophical itinerary is not a chronological accident. The negative dialectic has an intrinsic vocation to bring aesthetics to its end. Here philosophy allows aesthetic experience to step in as that which halts the sublation in the moment of appearance.

Many of the arguments in Adorno's critique of metaphysics can also be found, and in a more radical form, in the work of Lévinas. For Lévinas, as it was for Adorno, the Holocaust is the biographical event that determines (on theoretical bases previously developed) the unmasking of the connection between metaphysics and violence. As with Adorno, the Nazis' extermination of the Jews imposes itself on his theory not only as a qualitatively unheard-of fact (perhaps Lévinas considers the rest less "extraordinary" than Adorno, since it is just another manifestation of the sinfulness of man) but for the meaning that it assumes as theoretically "grounded" and rationally planned. What in Adorno was the double significance of metaphysics as the thinking of the violent removal of the rights of the transient—but also the only place for the affirmation of these rights, in the reference to a transcendent promise of sublation—is expressed in Lévinas through the terminological distinction between metaphysics (which is rightfully the opening of the finite onto the infinite) and ontology (which is the knowledge of the general structures of Being, in respect to which the individual is nothing more than the example of a type, already in principle ready to be erased, killed, exterminated). In Lévinas there is also, against the violence of ontology, an appeal to the irreducibility of the individual, its "face." Reducing the other to an example of Being through the knowledge of its essence (according to Lévinas, this is also the "violent" sense of ontological fore-understanding in Heidegger) means more than just violating the rights of our equals. The ethical nature of the relation to the other is given by the fact that this relation is always asymmetrical and thus imposes a responsibility on us beyond every implicit or explicit contractual relation. The other is the face, and it warrants hospitality and respect because it is turned toward the infinite, its desire places it in relation with God, whose trace it therefore carries. Here the violent thinking of metaphysics is not contrasted with an appeal to pure brotherhood, to equal respect for the other, but rather the idea that the experience of Being, which one has originarily in the encounter with the other, is the experience of an infinite that imposes itself as "majesty," as "command and authority."[10]

If Adorno seems to think about an overcoming of metaphysics and philosophy itself in aesthetic experience, Lévinas—regardless of all evidence to the contrary—prefigures an end of metaphysics and of philosophy itself as the transition to religious experience. It is true that his work is, above and beyond Talmudic commentary, philosophical discourse; yet, it is difficult to imagine it as something other than a *preambulum fidei*, a "destruction of the history of ontology" that is much more radical and definitive than that which Heidegger proposed as his program in *Being and Time*.

In their symmetry, the outcomes of Adorno and Lévinas can be placed effortlessly within a familiar schema—that of the forms of Hegelian absolute spirit. Both endeavor to "revoke" Hegelian reconciliation by stopping the dialectic at a previous stage, be it art or religion. The return to a "previous" moment of the dialectic seems particularly evident in Lévinas: the departure from metaphysics as the reduction of the other to the same is sought through a restoration of the metaphysical *Grund* in its most originary form, and ultimately the most peremptory (and, at least in this sense, most violent) form of the Lord, of majesty and command. But is the relation with this majesty really less violent than the metaphysical "foundation"? Might it not be an authentic experience of the sacred (for example, we can think of René Girard's thesis) that the first secularization—that is, the first step on the way toward the reduction of violence—must be carried to its end through a further secularization?

It seems less clear that even for Adorno the overcoming of metaphysics should be sought through the withdrawal to a previous stage of the Hegelian movement of absolute spirit. Nevertheless, there are many indications that it could be. First of all, what appears paradoxical for an avant-garde apologist like Adorno is his fundamentally "classicist" conception of the beautiful and aesthetic experience. In fact, for Adorno the justification of the avant-garde's revolt against the art of the past is pursued not so much out of the need to overcome the traditional experience of the beautiful—such as the "fullness" of the work of art, its structural perfection—as out of the will to defend an ideal of sublation, of harmony, and therefore of perfection and completion, if only in a utopian sense. This revolt stands against the phantasmogoric degeneration of art in the epoch when the market reigns supreme. This still profoundly classicist conception of the beautiful and aesthetic experience is but the revelatory symptom of a more general feature in Adorno's thought, namely, that regardless of the emphasis on micrology and appearance, the negative dialectic still conceives of the task of thought in relation to a telos that is always defined in terms of presence, of achieved sublation, of a "fullness" of Being. But is not the unfolded presence of Being—as achieved sublation no less than as authority, majesty, and command—what constitutes the violence of metaphysics?

Just as the objections to metaphysics are not principally motivated by "reasons of conscience," that is, by pure and simple theoretical insufficiencies, so too the greater or lesser resoluteness of the overcoming proposed by Adorno or by Lévinas is not measured merely in terms of internal contradictions or the aporetic nature of their theses. The effort to point out, in theoretical terms, the limits and the aporias in the Adornian and Lévinasian positions produces the vague feeling that these two thinkers, each in his own way, "leave out" too many elements integral to the problem of the overcoming of metaphysics as the thinking linked to violence. The religious conversion that, without a doubt, represents Lévinas's final word and the recourse to aesthetic experience that seems to conclude the itinerary of Adorno's critical thought nonetheless evoke Heidegger's words in *What Is Called Thinking?* concerning the uselessness of humanity's "interventions" or "decisions" unless Being reveals (gives) itself in ways different than those that marked the destiny of metaphysics.[11] Certainly, even the almost overly emphatic attitude of "anticipation" and "listening" seems to offer little for dealing with the problems that thought faces. Heidegger, however, in respect not only to Adorno and Lévinas but also to many other perspectives on the renewal of metaphysics, has a problematic advantage in that he explicitly poses the problem regarding the belonging of thought and the subject to a historical horizon, a horizon of destiny, from which one cannot escape through an appeal to some originary experience. Religious conversion and the recourse to aesthetic experience are two solutions that still place the subject at the center of the decision. In the case of Lévinas, the decision is overly dominated by the ideals of force implied in the very idea of the infinite. And for Adorno, on the opposite side, the decision is too weak, as it ties itself to the mere appearance of the beautiful. In both cases, however, the departure from violence and the overcoming of metaphysics depend on the ability of the subject to gain access to an originary experience, in some sense not compromised, an experience that retains many features of metaphysics. In fact, it continues to function as the means of access to a *Grund* by virtue of which, almost deductively, thought should "transform" by placing itself in a dimension of authenticity.

Heidegger tries to exit this schema by taking leave from humanism, insisting on anticipation and listening rather than on decision and conversion and, above all in the later writings, through his conception of the *Ge-stell*. This term ought to be translated as "en-framing" in order to respect Heidegger's intention to grant the German word, which literally means "scaffolding," the significance of the gathering (*Ge-*) of the *Stellen* (to place, to arrange, to order, to compose, and so on). According to Heidegger, this indicates the nature of the techno-scientific world in which we live today. More or less, it deals with the world of total administration of which Adorno speaks, and that, again in harmony with Adorno (not recognized, however, by either of them), Heidegger sees as the realization of metaphysics. Metaphysics, in fact, is ideally directed toward enclosing everything within the schema of the principle of sufficient reason, such that it carries everything back to explicit connections of foundation and completely realizes this program through the fundamentally unlimited dissemination of technology guided by modern experimental science. In contrast to Adorno's conclusion, the realization of metaphysics in the *Ge-stell* is for Heidegger not a mere "parody" that should be contrasted with the revoking of false sublation that takes the dialectical movement back to a preceding moment, such as that of aesthetic appearance. If thought has a *chance* to go beyond metaphysics and the violence connected to it, this *chance* is tied to the very movement of the *Ge-stell*, within which thought is totally lost, as in its destiny. The *Ge-stell* is that destinal horizon that does not allow an escape through a religious conversion or the contemplation of the appearance of the beautiful. Only if the *Ge-stell* is distorted or transformed in some way will Being reveal itself again (as in *What Is Called Thinking?*) and can we hope to be led beyond metaphysics.

With this conception of the *Ge-stell*, we return to the globality, and even the ambiguity, of the Nietzschean conception of the relation between metaphysics and violence. In its self-showing, the relation places thought in a condition that no longer allows it to think in terms of conversion or even in terms of originary experience. Heidegger, in a context that raises this very question of the connection between overcoming metaphysics and the *Ge-stell*, expresses this condition by rejecting the notion that metaphysics can be considered an error that, recognized for what it is, is dropped like a bad habit. This is understood, first of all, in the sense that Heidegger grants it in the pages of his essay on humanism where he speaks of the missing follow-up to *Being and Time* due to the metaphysical "remnants" tied to the language of philosophy, survivors that cannot be liquidated solely by terminological and linguistic devices; but it is also understood in the sense that denies metaphysics a new beginning, since this would always risk the possibility of accepting another foundation, another truth that would merely replace an old form of metaphysical thinking with a new one that functions in the same way. Thus the transition of intellectual hegemony in advanced societies from "philosophers," or even from humanistic intellectuals, to the scientists (who practice on everything else a hegemony much less illusory, one that perhaps conforms to the fact that, in the *Ge-stell*, metaphysics is "realized" by conferring a weight of new reality even on the hegemony of knowledge, which in the times of traditional metaphysics was largely ideological) is still a rebirth of metaphysics, even if in a "final" form that conforms to the *Ge-stell*.

One cannot exit the *Ge-stell* through a renewed access to some originary experience, not even disguised in the garb of scientific knowledge and the new hegemony of the scientists. This, however, confers a profound ambiguity on Heidegger's notion of the *Ge-stell* that conceals both the risks of his position and its positive importance, namely, the ability to speak of the overcoming of metaphysics and the violence connected to it in terms that are not purely aporetic.

The development of the problems in *Being and Time*—which already began from motives irreducible to merely *erkenntnistheoretisch* terms—led Heidegger to an ever-more radical "eventualization of the existentials,"[12] that is, to the recognition that everything that still appears in the "existentialistic" reflection of *Being and Time* as the constitution of existence (even if already clearly distinct from the "categories" through which entities or things in the world are given) is carried back to the *event* of Being. The existential analytic does not speak of essential human traits but of the ways of happening (of *wesen*, of "essentializing") of the Dasein of humanity in the epoch into which we are thrown, the epoch of completed metaphysics. Every claim to oppose a *Verfassung* (an originary or natural constitution of existence, or even an authentic experience of the pure structures of Being) to fallenness (the inauthentic existence of average everydayness) or to the destiny of humanity in the age of metaphysics or technology and social rationalization does nothing but remain within the epoch where various "first principles" have hierarchically structured the phases of Western history. They deal with the various configurations of Nietzsche's "true world," which in *Twilight of the Idols* is transformed into a "fable."[13]

The growing awareness of all of this—namely, the clearly nihilistic bearing of the critique of the idea of Being as presence and the attempt to think it radically as event—leads Heidegger to see the destiny of Being in the *Ge-stell*. As already noted, metaphysics is also for Heidegger the thinking that ends in the (fundamentally) total rationalization of the world; but, precisely as such, it is also that event in the course of which, in the end, "there is nothing to Being itself" (*es mit dem Sein selbst nichts mehr ist*).[14] Being is completely dissolved in the subjugation of all beings by the power available to technology, a power that always ends up turning against the subject as well (conforming to the critical descriptions of alienation), who thus becomes an "available" element of the *Ge-stell*'s universal imposition. Yet here, where both Being and humanity are involved in the development of the *Ge-stell*,[15] there also resides the possibility that the *Ge-stell* represents not only the final moment of metaphysics, but the first step toward its overcoming. The unfolding of metaphysics in the world of total techno-scientific availability makes the thinking of Being as foundation impossible (since the foundation is completely transformed in sufficient reason, whose founding force is inseparable from the will of the subject who discovers, manipulates, calculates, and utilizes it). But this very fact excludes the possibility that thought, once it undertakes this dissolution of the foundation, can stir up another "foundation" (originary experience, aesthetic appearance, divine majesty) in order to begin from the top. If there is a *chance* for a new beginning, it cannot rest in the possibility that the subject turns to a new principle by remaining in the schema of the relation between the human as subject and Being as objective principle, as *gegen-stand*, which stands before us as something that can be returned to after the error, the forgetting, the turning away.

But the *Ge-stell* could be distorted, and Being once again could turn itself beyond the forgetting and the dissolution of metaphysics. This carries important consequences both on the ontological level and on the "historical" level. Being that possibly reveals itself again, leading thought beyond the metaphysical forgetfulness, can no longer bear the features of the principle, of authority, of the foundation that belonged to the metaphysical tradition, since both the givenness of these characteristics and their dissolution are not "merely" errors of humanity (the subject facing a being-object, "from the outside") but the destiny of Being itself. On the "historical" level, this radical mode of overcoming metaphysics will mean a particular capacity to gather the announcement of a new existence outside of the violence that belongs to the age of metaphysics, in the unfolding of the society of total rationalization. It is in the *Ge-stell*, even as mass society, where the only chances for an overcoming of the inauthenticities characteristic of our history are.

Here we face two of the most problematic and even scandalous features of Heideggerian thought: his insistence on the overcoming of metaphysics, not through a human initiative, but through Being itself and its destiny; and second, the subsequent acceptance of modern social rationalization and of massification, which Adorno had perhaps exaggerated in his critique of Heidegger but which is nevertheless undeniable—regardless of the many signs to the contrary (the "archaism" of Heidegger, his disdain for science and technology).[16] A discussion of Adorno's objections, which capture the essential elements of the Heideggerian position even if he misunderstands them, allows us to clarify that the Heideggerian meditation of the *Ge-stell* contains important indications for completing the discourse on the overcoming of metaphysics as the thinking of violence.

Heidegger's antihumanism, his placing of the destiny of humanity on the destiny of Being, in Adorno's eyes seems to be an illusory satisfaction of the "ontological need" that emerges in contemporary humanity as the need to save, in any way, the substantiality of the I in a world where everything is reduced to a relation of functions. In the view of Adorno, Heidegger opposes a philosophy of Being to the system of functional relations, a philosophy that is much more insightful and efficacious the more it gathers Being beyond every possible endeavor of the subject in a destinal ordering that seems to furnish a solid guarantee, but that, to the very degree that by definition it removes every human initiative and decision, comes to an end in an implicit apology for the existing order. To Heidegger's apparent falling back into objectivity (inspired by an antisubjectivism that, we must remember, is motivated by the need to provide a solid ground, which cannot be sought in the subject impoverished by universal functionalism), Adorno opposes a dialectical ideal of freedom that places itself outside of the subject-object dichotomy, with which Heidegger's critique also took issue. But as is clear from the arguments in the pages dedicated to the "ontological need" in *Negative Dialectics*, for Adorno the Heideggerian overturning threatens the free subject precisely insofar as it is conceived as the principle of unlimited self-determination that sets itself against the object as a purely antithetical term, as the material of its domination. Only from the point of view rigidly attached to the juxtaposition of subject and object can the Heideggerian effort to overcome metaphysics by appealing to a destiny of Being appear as a pure overturning in objectivity. It is true, as Adorno writes in these pages, that "the history accumulated in subjects" forbids thought a sharp turn toward positions that, believing themselves to be radical, are but a wandering in the emptiness—like certain migrations toward the East, Zen Buddhism, and so on.[17] But the history of Western subjectivity entails more experiences than those gathered in Adorno's work. That is why the subject that he sees threatened by the overturning of Heidegger is only the dialectical subject not yet overcome, either through the existential analytic of Heidegger or even through Nietzsche's critique.

Is the violent nature of metaphysics really, as Adorno sees it, the death of freedom and of the rights of the sovereign subject—the modern subject, for which the reconciliation with the other than oneself coincides with a nonalienated praxis, namely, an unlimited one like the will to power—or, rather, will we be able to suspect that it begins and already has roots where Being unfolds in the contentious juxtaposition between subject and object? If the *Ge-stell* contains a *chance* for the overcoming of metaphysics in the act of stripping the human of his qualities as a subject, Adorno has no doubt that this qualification—in the name of a cultural memory that we must not betray, but that he even limits drastically—has to be defended and affirmed. There is nothing to make him doubt its "validity," which is only practically threatened by total organization. If we are aware of this difference, it will also be clear that while Heidegger's attitude in the face of the *Ge-stell* ought to appear to Adorno like an apology for that very form of existence inspired by metaphysics that becomes a real parody, it in fact deals with overcoming. To a certain degree, Adorno makes sense: Heidegger sees the *Ge-stell* as a destiny, even in the sense that only from it can one expect, beyond the "height of danger," a maturation into "that which saves" (according to Hölderlin's verse cited by Heidegger). If we can no longer believe—since precisely this is forbidden by the unveiling of the connection between metaphysics and violence—that we can appeal to an originary or a different foundation in the form of an aesthetics of appearance or in the form of the majesty of the Lord, then the call that signals the overcoming of metaphysics, by revealing the impossibility of its continuation, must come from metaphysics itself and from its world. If we want to give a plausible meaning to the page (almost the only one) where Heidegger speaks of the *Ge-stell* as "the first lighting of the Ereignis,"[18] we can begin only from the Heideggerian observation that the *Ge-stell* strips humanity and Being "of those determinations given to them by metaphysics," namely, those qualities of subject and object.[19] Both Heidegger and Adorno agree that metaphysics, in a profound way, has pushed violence to its extreme in the world of total organization. But Heidegger goes far beyond this recognition. One cannot attribute to Heidegger the various attempts—beyond the most philosophically distinct ones from Adorno and Lévinas that are under discussion here—to imagine an overcoming of metaphysics through the restoration of previous stages in its development by returning to the moments in which it was not yet dissolved or realized in technology. Such is the case with a certain archaism widespread in Italian philosophy over the past few decades (Emanuele Severino) that is often connected to a philosophy of tragedy inspired by Schelling, Nietzsche, and Heidegger

(Massimo Cacciari), but also to the continuation of the Enlightenment project by Jürgen Habermas or the Kantian one by Dieter Henrich. For Heidegger the realization of metaphysics in the *Ge-stell* makes similar returns "impossible." The *Ge-stell* cannot be exorcized by looking to recover, in an illusory way, some infancy or adolescence of thinking—given the destiny that metaphysics has already had, which was a matter of a destiny (not of an error or an arbitrary choice of humanity), the recovery of its previous stages might lead us somewhere other than where we currently are. The *Ge-stell* is traversed—namely, lived out as the destiny of the experience of the dissolution of the subject who was placed there by the world into which it was thrown. Not, however, due to a dialectical faith in the overturning of extreme negativity in positivity, as if the total absence of Being and the subject were a guarantee for a presence yet to be restored (metaphysics would therefore disguise itself as nihilism only in order to rise again gloriously—powerfully, violently, in a new "evidence"). The thinking and the existence of an "after metaphysics" take shape only by following the "dissolutive" way indicated by the *Ge-stell*: humanity and Being must lose, definitively, and not for the time being, the feature that constitutes them in metaphysics—that of the subject and of the object. The "essential word" that Heidegger always sought, even in his unrelenting return to the dawning moments of European philosophy, is perhaps much closer to the daily chatter of the late-modern world than to the arcane silence of the mystic and the sacred experience.

Heidegger did not follow this path, despite having opened it with his vision of the *Ge-stell*. It would therefore be excessive, at least if one sticks to the letter of the texts, to read, for example, the page from *On the Way to Language*[20] regarding the "simple silencing of the silence" as the only "authentic saying" in the sense of an invitation to "let Being go" not only as *Grund*,[21] but also as the silent essential word. Yet it is on this path that one must move forward, with Heidegger and beyond him, even beyond the letter of his texts, if one is to remain faithful to his program of preparing a new coming of Being by corresponding to the call of the *Ge-stell*. It is difficult that this call—to depart from meta-physics, and primarily from its basic schema, the opposition between subject and object—points only in the direction of a recognition of the intersubjective constitution of the subject itself, as in Habermas's *Theory of Communicative Action*. Habermas rightly takes distance from Adorno by noting that these remain tied to a metaphysical conception of the subject, but Habermas himself, in his turn, also remains oriented toward the construction of a normative structure of the "socialized sub-ject"; and since its intersubjectivity provides it with a suprahistorical constitution, it is not contaminated by the idea of "destiny," of sending, of constant belonging to an event. With that, the "advantage" of dis-carding the self-centered metaphysical subject ends up rather deficient, or even brings with it the risk of a restorative overturning.[22] Despite all of his claims to the contrary, the path taken by Habermas, and by Karl-Otto Apel with his notion of unlimited communication, is nev-ertheless an example of how one should not proceed after metaphysics, lest the subject be consumed. The *Ge-stell* (seen even in Habermas as the society of "roles," and for which, after Max Weber, the reference to the experience of interactionalism within American society is deci-sive) makes the subject as self-centered I unthinkable, though yet again, even the imposition of communicative action as a transcendental norm thwarts this beginning and tries to exorcise the dissolution whose con-tinuation was at issue.

One departs from metaphysics and the violence connected to it by letting it recall—and not only negatively—the dissolution that the *Ge-stell* places upon the subject and the object of metaphysics. Only Heidegger has presented the many aspects of this dissolution. For example, he has not explicitly thematized the dissolution of the objec-tivity of the subjects determined by the *Ge-stell* to the degree that the technology that characterizes it is no longer only that of mechanical force (the motor and, at its extreme, atomic energy are the great exam-ples that Heidegger presents when he speaks of technology) but that of collecting, organizing, and distributing information.[23]

Does all of this, however, not mean remaining precisely within the world of completed metaphysics, abandoning it all to the *Ge-stell*, accepting it and, as Adorno says, making a more or less explicit apology for it? But is there (still) a *Ge-stell*? Conceiving of the ontology of Heidegger as a new deterministic metaphysics that confers upon Being (in the form of the technological destiny of the late-modern world) the preeminence over human endeavors means developing yet again a relation of "foundation" between the "true world" (the laws of the destiny of Being that Heidegger mentions) and the "apparent world" (history, society, human existence); yet, it is precisely a question of the dissolution of this distinction. Heidegger's would be a deterministic ontology if he were to affirm the primacy of the object over the subject. Then it would be a matter of defending subjectivity against the monstrous domination of the structures of universal objectification, as seen in Adorno. But the *Ge-stell* that removes the meaning from the juxtaposition of subject and object no longer lets it be thought as the true world, as the necessary structure from which one "deduces" the destiny of humanity. It is the gathering of the *Stellen*—the technological civilization in which the world is nothing (more) than the web of "world pictures,"[24] and the subject just the geometrical site of a multiplicity of roles that can never be fully unified, history itself a sort of constellation of the multiple (and not unifiable) reconstructions that historiography and chronicle give to them. It is impossible to configure *Ge-stell* as the foundation of an "objective" necessity that imposes itself upon the subject by limiting its freedom. This impossibility is the true end of metaphysics—which manifests itself, therefore, as the end of philosophical discourse as "hegemon"—that culminates in the technological organization of the world. Heidegger invites us to listen for and to await the renewed call of Being, which no longer speaks in the form of the *arché*, of the grounding principle, of the essential structure, or even as the intersubjective constitution of existence. The "true world" is now a fable. A certain "crumbling" or fraying of Heidegger's philosophical discourse after *Being and Time* can also be said to mark its stylistic expression. If Being speaks, it takes the form of a general buzzing, a polyphony of sounds, a murmuring, and perhaps even the form of the "neuter" whose announcement Maurice Blanchot says we ought to expect.

"To tolerate a good deal of chance" (Nietzsche); or "to let go of Being as foundation" (Heidegger); or even "to encourage a certain degree of frivolity when dealing with traditional philosophical questions" (Rorty)[25]—these are the ways in which one can describe the philosophical discourse open to the call of the *Ge-stell*. Could it mean, according to Adorno's condemnation, simply and cynically abandoning oneself to the alienating course of things? The alternative—which Adorno never explicitly embraces—would be to cut the link between metaphysics, rationalization, and violence through an extreme and "ultimate" act of violence, a recurring dream found in some of the highest moments of twentieth-century philosophy, from Benjamin to Sartre. Nietzsche and Heidegger, on the other hand, propose a path of "moderation" and of listening, one that does not present the schema of foundation again and again, but resigns itself to it, accepts it as destiny, distorts it, and secularizes it.

10 FROM HEIDEGGER TO MARX

Hermeneutics as the Philosophy of Praxis

With increasing clarity, even for the *Wirkungsgeschichte* of years that separate us from the first edition of Gadamer's inaugural work (*Warheit und Methode*, 1960), it becomes apparent that hermeneutics cannot be called anything but a (*the?*) philosophy of praxis. Now, this is the term that Antonio Gramsci used in his *Prison Notebooks* to indicate Marx's philosophy. Perhaps it was only a matter of avoiding the name of the founder of communism in writings that could have been inspected by his guards. It was, however, a very suitable term, *sachlich*, conforming to the content to which he was referring. And so, this expression applies fundamentally to hermeneutics, more than it ever did to Marxism. We can say more than it did to Marxism because insofar as Marxism still retained a trace of metaphysical belief in the "necessary" course of history, it could not be considered a radical philosophy of praxis. It is with this in mind that it seems reasonable to consider the hermeneutics that follows, and for me that means a nihilistic hermeneutics, as the antimetaphysical radicalization of Marxism.

The two distant roots from which Gadamerian, and initially Heideggerian, hermeneutics originates are a religious one and a juridical-political one. The theory and practice of interpretation have always wanted to have something to do with the reading and the topical application of sacred or juridical texts, far more than with the reading of the literary tradition. And so, by finally being recognized—precisely in its nihilistic version—as a radical philosophy of praxis, hermeneutics fully recovers its religious origin and its political origin. Today, in fact, hermeneutics as the theory of the event of Being that is realized in every unforeseeable novelty of interpretations finds itself confronted by the dogmatic claims of the church, especially the Catholic church, no less than by the claims of dominant political powers. It seems a fate tied to the ubiquity of mass media and of forms of information: power today, whether religious or political, does not seem to be able to act without asserting dogmas and truth claims (Carl Schmitt's doctrine of friend-enemy is much better, as it would have never justified the extermination of entire populations with a theory of universal justice: we are the good, they are the evil empire). For this, whoever might assert—such as Nietzsche and radical hermeneutics—that "there are no facts, only interpretations" would more or less be considered a terrorist. And perhaps, in effect, that person is: he is a rebel who turns against every claim about the stability and legitimacy of the existing order, and defends the right to institute new orders founded solely on the common will. (That is also simply the essence of democracy.)

The connection of interpretation to praxis, which moreover dominates Gadamer's theory and its reference to Aristotle, is always considered in a way that is too reassuring. The novelty of interpretations as well as the epochal openings of Being—which Heidegger believes he recognizes principally in the happening of the work of art (the opening of a world and, please note, the "bringing forth" of earth)—cannot be attributed solely to the biological succession of generations: new human beings are born and carry with themselves a renewal of interpretations and thus make Being "happen" in new historical-destinal configurations. (Death is the casket of Being.) I have already noted elsewhere that in the essay on the work of art Heidegger also and in other ways alludes to the happening of truth beyond the work of art, and one of these is the founding of a state, for example. As we know, Heidegger did not develop this thesis, even though in the works following the essay from 1936 he is always looking for the event of Being in the work of poets ("But what remains is founded by the poets," Hölderlin), and that is perhaps understood by thinking of his political misadventure in 1933. But it is not difficult to try to take up his thought on this very point, also in light of the connection between interpretation and praxis that one finds clearly indicated by Gadamer. A new opening of Being is not given except as the birth of a new interpretation; but this does not fall from the sky—the work of the poets is also praxis, it is a doing that af-firms [af-ferma], that establishes a foundation, and that is not legitimated by any precedent. Does the grounding ungroundedness also have value for political action? Let us not deny that this is a problem for the critics who, as we were saying, identify radical hermeneuticians with "terrorists."[1] In the name of what do we start a revolution? In the name of what do we write a poem that will become a classic? Whether in the case of the classic or in the case of revolution it seems that only the result, the historical occurrence, is in play. The classic becomes what it is because "the public" reads it and recognizes it as such. Revolution succeeds if it is really declared, if it gives rise to institutions that meet with widespread participation. But natural right? "Truth" and "values"? What is called natural right is what the revolutionary invokes in order to sustain the participation of others, and thus to produce a post factum legitimization of his enterprise of transformation. I am listing these issues and am trying to offer these responses only to avoid hiding the difficulty of constructing a political action that grounds without being in its turn grounded. Whoever, with whatever good reason, withdraws when faced with these consequences of a radical hermeneutics must nonetheless reckon with all of the "lethal" implications of metaphysical positions: a politics grounded in "truth" can only be a politics of authority—philosophers, central committees, pontiffs. One might note that in the world of today we have to deal precisely with politicians who claim to be "true": right where the authority of "natural" law professed by popes is imposed, the "scientific" laws of economics show themselves to us.[2]

There is no natural right to revolution, no truth configurable in valid statements that justify the revolutionary act. Even in Marx, moreover, it was only a matter of the fact that the proletariat, reduced by capitalistic expropriation to the state of pure and simple *Gattungswesen*, "generic human essence," as such revolts and has with it the "right" of all those who have been reduced to this condition. Walter Benjamin, in his "Theses on the History of Philosophy" (one of his last writings, if not the last), writes (I am citing this from memory) that revolutionaries are inspired in their action much more by the memory of their exploited and oppressed ancestors than they are by the vision of a new human project they would like to make real. Only the spirit of vengeance, as Nietzsche would say? Or is something else here, what we can without much interpretative violence link to Heidegger's insistence on *An-denken*, "remembrance," as the only possible way to escape from the metaphysical forgetting of Being that was imposed by metaphysics and, namely, by the authoritarianism of the identification of Being with the current order of beings?

Won't the silence of Being to which Heidegger invites us to listen, outside of every mysticism-producing interpretation (from which Heidegger himself did not escape), be the silence belonging to the "losers" of history about whom Benjamin speaks? This is a hypothesis that would in a definite manner move us closer to the hermeneutics of the philosophy of praxis, namely, to Marxism as Gramsci called it. Taking leave of metaphysics, Heidegger says, is not possible in a radical way, and thus he speaks of a *Verwindung*, of a "distortion," rather than of an *Überwindung*, "an overcoming." Would a *Verwindung* be the revolution that Benjamin's communists aim to produce through the remembrance of exploited ancestors? To read it in this way, and not as the institution of a completely new order, seems unavoidable precisely in view of what have been the revolutions that are conceived as *Überwindungen*. As if to say, if Lenin and Stalin had known Heidegger and his *Verwindung*, would they have avoided producing the failures of real socialism that brought about the destruction of the Soviet

Union? I am formulating the question in the most paradoxical and radical manner because one understands what is at stake here. For the very reason that there is no truth that one might formulate metaphysically beyond concrete and contingent situations, this hypothesis does not make any sense and has the flavor of grotesque irony. However, the fact that *today* revolution appears readable in terms of *Verwindung* liberates a completely legitimate field of reading and of interpretation. It is *today* that we become aware of the proximity between the silence of Benjamin's losers and the silence of Heidegger's Being. It is today that, at the end of metaphysics in the nihilism of the mediatized world of global imperialism, we become aware that a revolution conceived as *Überwindung* can do nothing but give rise to new metaphysical configurations of domination.

Listening to the silence of Being would have seemed—and for some time has seemed to Marxists and anti-Heideggerians—like a pointless form of aestheticism. In Heidegger this appearance of mysticism-producing pointlessness is never completely gone. This can be attributed not only to his prudence after his adventure with Nazism, when he really believed that the nonmetaphysical civilization of pre-classical Greece could be reborn through the antimodernity and anticapitalism of the Nazis. Heidegger's reason for remaining in a mystical-poetic listening to the voice of Being up to his last days can perhaps also be read in his diffidence toward the new metaphysical configuration that was imposed, after the Second World War, by the Allied rebuilders of democracy: the claim by the judges at Nuremberg to represent natural law and the universal idea of justice, the persistent conviction of the Western powers that they were the empire of the good; the "free world," as the "Voice of America," proclaimed across the planet for a long time on radio. To accept all of this as final was not only—as it appeared to many who had fought under the banner of Italian fascism, for example—jumping onto the bandwagon of the winners; for Heidegger it represented a real betrayal of ontological difference, a relapse into the error of 1933.

Working for revolution without falling back into metaphysics is the task of hermeneutics as the philosophy of praxis and the way for any emancipation here in the world of the end of metaphysics and of accomplished nihilism. Heidegger's insistence on *An-denken*, "remembrance," far from being a nostalgic attitude, here becomes the source for every legitimization of transformative action. There is no truth lest it be in the dialogue between humans; it is in dialogue that Being happens. And this dialogue nevertheless demands that we listen to those who for a long time have been silenced by the structures of domination. Calling upon the excluded to speak is the only nonmystical, nonmystifying way to listen to the voice of Being beyond the metaphysics that confuses it with the given order of beings.

A hermeneutic humanism, similar to the one proposed here, must be constructed in the *Gespräch*, according to the expression from Hölderlin repeated many times by Heidegger. But dialogue, the conversation between humans in which, solely, Being happens, demands the listening to silence—the silence of that Being that metaphysics and the society of domination have always hidden and silenced—or rather the soft voice of the excluded, of history's defeated. Completely different than a passive listening, as is appears. A hermeneutic humanism cannot in the end be anything but a revolutionary humanism.

THE END OF PHILOSOPHY IN
THE AGE OF DEMOCRACY

When discussing the current role of philosophy in our late-modern or postmodern societies, it is perhaps useful to underline the analogies that exist between books such as Karl Popper's *The Open Society and Its Enemies* and the ideas Heidegger discusses in many of his works, particularly in a lecture such as "The End of Philosophy and the Task of Thinking" from 1964. This is obviously a paradoxical approach, above all because Heidegger does not at all seem to be a passionately "democratic" thinker. And yet the reasons that push Popper to oppose Plato are fundamentally the same reasons that motivate Heidegger in his polemic against metaphysics, which, as he writes specifically in the opening of that lecture, is always Platonism, from antiquity all the way to Kant, Hegel, and Nietzsche. If, in fact, we write the Heideggerian term *Ereignis*, "event," in place of Popper's expression "open society," we do not betray the intentions of either Popper or Heidegger, even if neither of them would agree with this small hermeneutic act of "violence."

Popper maintains that Plato was a dangerous enemy of the open society because he had an essentialistic conception of the world: everything that is real conforms to a law that is given as the structure of Being, and society must not do anything but compare itself to this essential order. Since philosophers are those who know the essential order of things, the control of society is up to them. The function that is attributed to philosophers—or, rather, today, scientists, technicians, experts— over the centuries, that of supreme advisors to princes, is closely tied to this fundamental conviction: for both the individual and society, corresponding to an objectively given order also functions as the only possible moral norm. A modern principle such as the one according to which "*auctoritas, non veritas, facit legem*" was always exposed to the rationalistic critique derived from metaphysics, even when this was motivated by the best revolutionary intentions. In politics, wherever the truth is in play, there is also the danger of authoritarianism, that is, of the "closing" that Popper stigmatizes in his work.

Now, what Heidegger calls "metaphysics" is precisely the idea of Being as an objectively given order once and for all for everyone; Nietzsche also reproached Socrates for this, seeing in him the initiator of modern decadence, which killed the great tragic spirit of the ancient Greeks. If Being is a structure given once and for all for everyone, one can think neither an opening of history nor one of freedom. Naturally, a vision like this is more reassuring than the tragic one typical of the dawn of Greek thinking; but the reassurance, we will be able to add, matters above all for those who are already secure in the existing order, and for this, above all, they recognize it as rational and worthy of having value forever. (I am thinking here, beyond Nietzsche, of Benjamin's "Theses on the Philosophy of History.") I remember that, in the same opening pages of the lecture on the end of philosophy, Heidegger cites the name of Karl Marx right next to Plato's, as he was someone who had already enacted, before Nietzsche, the overturning of metaphysics and thus of Platonism. By this I do not mean that one might be able to bridge completely the gap between the Marxist overturning and the "overcoming" (*Überwindung*) about which Heidegger himself was thinking. But surely it is not arbitrary on our part to think also about Marx's ideas on the origins of alienation in the social separation of labor when we try to understand, with Heidegger, why and how metaphysics is established in such a radical way in the history of our world.

I will leave aside the question of the "historical" or "eternal" character of metaphysics in Heidegger's thought, which would lead to the development of a discourse on his never overcome, and perhaps unavoidable, dependence on the biblical myth of original sin.

Even if the notion of metaphysics is used by Heidegger in a rather peculiar way, I believe that the analogy with Popper, however paradoxical, might be able to clarify in what sense it is also shared by the greater part of contemporary philosophy; certainly it would not be difficult to recognize it in Wittgenstein,[1] and obviously in pragmatism and neopragmatism. Whether they are disciples of classical thought and the neoscholastic tradition or of that peculiar neoscholasticism that is surely analytic philosophy—in which ontology, metaphysics, and the like indicate only the structures of knowledge established in "regional ontologies," by now deprived of that elasticity and historicity that were still able to be recognized in the transcendental categories of Kant and even of Husserl—I know well that they still speak about metaphysics in a way that agrees terminologically. In the end, however, it is clear enough, at least in the greater part of contemporary philosophy, that the Heideggerian idea of metaphysics as the identification of true Being with an unchanging structure, objectively recognizable and the source of norms, is widely shared and rejected on the theoretical level, even if not under the name of its principle author.

Beginning with this very refusal of metaphysics understood in this way—a refusal that can be motivated by Nietzschean-Heideggerian reasons, or by reasons derived from Wittgenstein, Carnap, or Popper—one can legitimately pose the problem of the end of philosophy in the age of democracy. In fact, by going well beyond Heidegger and Popper, one can simply equate the end of philosophy as metaphysics with the affirmation, practical and political, of democratic regimes. Where there is democracy, there cannot be a class of the holders of the "true" truth who either exercise power directly (the philosopher-kings of Plato) or provide the sovereign with rules for his behavior. For this, I repeat, the reference to Marx from Heidegger's aforementioned lecture seems to me symptomatic. These same pages discuss the end of metaphysics due to the dissolution that it endures in the specialization of the individual sciences, from psychology to sociology to anthropology, or from logic to logistics and semantics, all the way to cybernetics (what today we instead call computer science).

As it is understood, this is not at all an abstract argument: those among us who teach philosophy in schools and universities experience this progressive dissolution of philosophy every day. In the universities where they establish new courses in psychology, anthropology, informational science, the numbers enrolled in philosophy courses drop off dramatically. And the resources made available to those who study philosophy also diminish. Certainly, all of this is correct and inevitable, even if it is unpleasant for many of us and above all for our students. It is, however, a very concrete example of the "end of philosophy," which seems to not have anything to do with democracy directly, being tied only to the growing autonomy of the human sciences. But, as Heidegger also points out, it corresponds to a growing power and social prestige of specialists, who are accompanied by an ever-greater "scientific" control over the various aspects of shared life.

If one accounts for all of that, one also sees that the end of philosophy leaves behind a hole that democratic societies cannot ignore. On the one side, namely, philosophy understood as the sovereign function of knowers in the governing of the polis is dead and buried. On the other side, as the title of Heidegger's lecture on the "task of thinking" after the end of philosophy-metaphysics suggests, there remains the specifically democratic problem of avoiding the substitution of the authority of the philosopher-king with the unchecked power of technicians in the various sectors of social life. We are dealing with a power still more dangerous because it is more underhanded and fragmented—so much so that the revolutionary aim of "hitting the heart of the state" becomes absurd, since power is objectively distributed among the many centers that tend to the various specializations. If we wish to use a psychological metaphor, I would say that there is the risk of constructing a schizophrenic society, where again and again a new supreme power is established, that of doctors, of nurses, of straightjackets and caged beds.

Let us therefore try to modify the title of Heidegger's lecture in this way: "the end of philosophy in democratic societies and the (political) task of thinking." The sovereign role of the philosopher has ended because sovereigns have come to an end. It is not easy to say if these "ends" might be tied to a relation of cause and effect. Like Marx, Heidegger would also say that the end of metaphysics, and thus of the philosopher's claim to sovereignty, is not a matter that is completed first of all due to the work of philosophers. Certainly, for him all of this is instead an event of Being to which the philosopher must only co-respond. But, as one sees, the distance from Marx ends up being very relative: where does the Being to which the philosopher must respond speak? Not in the economic-material "structure" of society, for sure, at least not only and exclusively in it. But Heidegger's call not to be satisfied with the "present and the existing presenting of what is present" recalls, and not just superficially, the Marxist critique of ideology, the "school of suspicion" that, for example, is expressed in a maxim from Brecht: "Because things are the way they are, things will not stay the way they are."[2]

For us even the possibility of advancing interpretative proposals that are still relatively scandalous but that thirty years ago would have been unthinkable—hypothesizing the proximity of Popper's open society and the end of metaphysics as considered by Heidegger—is not born from any philosophical discovery, but, if it has any validity, is in its turn a response to the new conditions of the age. In relation to the moment in which Popper and Heidegger were situated, the world today is much further down the road of integration and scientific rationalization; and the end of philosophy—both in the sense of its dissolution in the particular sciences and in the sense of the emptiness and the lack that it leaves in democracy itself—is a fact much more visible and universal. By proposing the thesis of the proximity of Popper and Heidegger, we did not discover a deeper truth, as this in fact would still be a form of metaphysical thought with the pretense of being absolute. Rather we

are corresponding to what happens, to the event—even in the specifically Heideggerian sense of the term.

The task of thinking in this situation—whether we refer back to
Heidegger or to Marx, maybe not to Popper—is to think what remains
hidden in the "everyday presentation" of that which always happens.
For Marx, this is the dialectical concreteness of the connections hidden
by ideology; for Heidegger, this is truth as *alétheia*, as the opening of
a horizon (or of a paradigm) that makes possible every truth understood as the conformity to things, verification or falsification of propositions. Naturally, Popper can no longer accompany us on this next
step of the discourse because the allusion to Marx or to a "hidden" that
is to be thought seems to take us far from the idea of an open society.
It would take too long to show that Popper's proximity with Heidegger and Marx in the terms I proposed can still work. Let us therefore
leave Popper behind. The approach of Marx and Heidegger, which the
latter suggests in the lecture about which I have been commenting,
nonetheless remains decisive. But is it possible to speak of the hidden
alétheia alluded to by Heidegger as if it were the concreteness of Marx's
economic-social relations? In other terms, how does the task of thinking take shape after the end of philosophy, when the philosophers no
longer think they have privileged access to ideas and essences, which
would put them in a position to govern or give rules to the sovereign? If
one were to follow Marx exclusively, we would return to a rationalistic
and historicistic metaphysics, in which the philosophers are given the
task of expressing the definitive truth of the history that only the expro-
priated proletariat knows and realizes with revolution. Not even Marx,
in the end, really knew to look at Being as event; and on this count
Popper was right to consider him an enemy of the open society. If we
were to follow Heidegger exclusively, however, we would find ourselves
embroiled in that "unfounded mysticism, bad mythology, in any case
ruinous irrationalism" that he himself saw as a risk to which his position was exposed.[3] In order to avoid these dangers, which belong not
only to Heidegger but to much of philosophy today (at least those who

refuse becoming only an appendix—more or less superfluous—to the human sciences and the sciences in general), one must take a step forward on the path of that "urbanization of the Heideggerian precinct" inaugurated by Hans-Georg Gadamer (I am citing the by-now famous expression coined by Jürgen Habermas). Such an urbanization requires that Heidegger be liberated from "mysticism without foundation" by developing the reference to Marx beyond his intentions. In the essay "The Origin of the Work of Art" (1936), Heidegger indicated, among the various ways that truth happens, not only art but also the realms of religion, of ethics, of politics, and of "essential thinking." These indications remain undeveloped in the remainder of his thought. And moreover, here there is no question of remaining more or less faithful to his teaching, but also of searching for ways to solve our problem regarding the task and the future of philosophy after its end. In the age of the end of metaphysics, we can no longer seek out, as Heidegger did, the event of Being in those privileged moments to which his attention was always turned: the great poetic works, the "inaugural" words like Anaxamider's saying or Parmenides's poem, or the verses of Hölderlin. These texts still function as essences, as Platonic ideas, that only the philosophers recognize, and that once again give them "sovereign" voices. In the age of democracy, the event of Being toward which thought must turn its own attention is perhaps something much more widespread and less definite, perhaps closer to politics. The only term that can help us to think it is an expression from the later Foucault, which here, moreover, we take up in an autonomous way: the ontology of actuality. The event (of Being) to which thinking had the task of corresponding in the age of democracy is the way in which Being is configured one step at a time in collective experience. The hidden that tends to escape into the specialization of the sciences is the *on he on*, Being as Being, the integral nature of individual and social experience that is subjected to the technological schizophrenia and the subsequent relapse into authoritarianism. To speak here of ontology and to entrust this task—yet again—to the "philosophers," no longer sovereigns or the advisors of sovereigns, certainly means imagining a new and yet to be defined role for the intellectual—not the scientist, not the technician, but something closer to a priest or an artist: the priest without hierarchy, however, or the street artist. Less imaginatively, one can think about a figure that has much to do with history and with politics, one that does some ontology in that he reconnects current experiences to those from the past, in a continuity that is the fundamental sense of the term logos—discourse—and that also constructs continuity in the community by helping the formation of increasingly new ways of being understood (Habermas spoke of the philosopher as *Dolmetscher*). *Does all of this really have anything to do with Being?* one might ask. I would respond: is Being perhaps something different, something deeper and more lasting and more hidden, than its "event"?

12

TRUE AND FALSE UNIVERSALISM

Generally we tie the crisis of the concept of universal truth and of the universalism that corresponds to it to the "epistemological" realization of the limits of rationality. We have become more guarded in our claims about what we know to be the true and definitive essence of things. Wittgenstein taught us that every proposition can claim validity only within a specific *language game*; Jaspers and Dewey taught us that the true is "what is good for us"; and Heidegger brought to light that every experience of truth is an experience of interpretation, and that the interpretation can never claim to be the faithful reflection of "reality," whatever such a term might mean. Even philosophers who are aware of this transformation of the concept of truth—who still are not many, since many of the most diverse schools of thought continue to think in terms of truth as the conformity of thought to the thing—more often than not stop at this epistemological level of the problem. It is as if there were, in the end, a history of truth that finally reached a phase of more "realistic" awareness of the limits of knowledge. And this awareness is still again thought more or less explicitly as a truth "more true" than the one believed by realists and objectivists of every sort, a truth that would be worthy of acceptance by all, and thus fundamentally still endowed with a legitimate claim to universality. As such, albeit paradoxically, the affirmation of the impossibility of a universal truth clashes with the claim to universality from numerous other doctrines: philosophical, religious, juridical. Ultimately it is just the umpteenth version of the antiskeptical argument: if one says that everything is false, one still claims to be correct and thus to state a truth, and everything that comes with that. Let us remember all of antiquity's reaction to Zeno's argument against motion: get up and begin to walk. The analogy here serves to show that one cannot argue in a logically (con)vincing way against the antiskeptical argument. It can only be overcome by practically changing the game. In our case, the critique of universalism cannot remain on the level of rational argumentation, as if it were a matter of getting the better of someone in a discussion. Nietzsche wrote, in an aphorism titled "An Affectation in Departing":[1] If one abandons a certain theoretical position, do not pretend to explain exhaustively why you have changed your mind. Even when you had embraced in the past the position that you now reject, you did not do it by providing theoretical arguments.

What I want to say is that philosophy, when confronted with the question of universalism, cannot remain on the level of theoretical argument—and in fact one finally realizes that what has kept it at this level has been the interests that, ideologically, it was always made to serve. In an essay that here serves as a guide,[2] Richard Rorty tried once and for all to retrace the origins of philosophy's claim to universality, correctly singling out a specific moment in the history of the Greek polis when, by expanding its own economic interests beyond the strict limits within which it traditionally operated, it was pushed—not necessarily by imperialistic motivations—to try to assert opinions that could win over the agreement of anyone who was not a citizen of the polis or Greek.

No matter how it might have been, we are accustomed to considering this "discovery" of universality as a positive step on the path to the "progress" of humanity and civilization. Still today, thinkers who we respect and hold in high regard such as Apel or Habermas think that one cannot make any assertion without defending, at least implicitly, its validity *erga omnes*. And these *omnes* are not only those who play our *language game*, or our fellow citizens, and so on; they are the universal audience of humanity, in front of whom our assertion claims validity in the name of Reason itself. As a consequence, in the vision of Habermas, there is no assertion, not even a limited one, that does not imply the acceptance of rationality as an inescapable background.

The relative "obviousness" with which theses such as these are presented, ultimately the idea that—almost naturally—every assertion ought to aim for universal validity, is probably an inheritance not only of rationalism (from the Greeks or the eighteenth century) but also of Christianity.

◆ ◆ ◆

For this reason one could consider providential, a *felix culpa*, the fact that today one often speaks, even if it is out of turn, of religious war: to expose the absurdity of those sorts of arguments means that one is not only more clearly aware of what is going on, by bringing an end to an error; it is also an occasion to clarify the meaning of religion in our world to the advantage of that same religious consciousness and with the result, one hopes, of offering a service to the various churches and religious denominations involved. Put in another way, to reflect on the question, and the untimeliness, of religious war in our world also means to begin to think in a more authentic way the universalism of the great religions of salvation on which modernity was constructed and that nourished the Western civilization under discussion here.

Certainly, one must not exaggerate the claim to recognize a providential direction in history. But it is nevertheless meaningful that the appearance of the clash of cultures—among the Christian, Jewish, and Muslim worlds—shows itself and is evoked today at least in the Christian world, but to some degree and in different forms also in the Jewish and Muslim worlds, such that the results of the secularization emerge in all of the breadth not only of religious traditions, but above all of the idea of truth itself. On this specific aspect of the question, it is also a matter of dispelling the many, and not always innocent, misunderstandings. To whomever speaks of the clash of civilizations and religious wars, it seems obvious that the Western, Christian world is today anything but equipped for such a conflict. Men of the church such as certain Italian bishops and cardinals who urge Catholics to defend Christian values against the spread of Islamic influence in Western Europe, or the appeals made by Western heads of state to the superiority of Christian civilization, which must be defended against terroristic barbarism—all of this shows clearly that, at least on the side of the Christian world, today one can speak about everything except the war of one religion against another. We are no longer material for society, Nietzsche wrote in *The Gay Science*. For sure, at least, we Westerners of today are no longer a society capable of fighting a religious war—thank God, one might say. If we recognize that, another question immediately arises: should we for this reason consider ourselves less authentically religious than our ancestors who undertook the crusades, who thought they were in this way fulfilling a sacred duty to God? I believe that few really think like this—except the cardinals and bishops and presidents mentioned above. Without necessarily criminalizing our ancestors—nevertheless knowing that even their religious motives were not as exclusive and dominating as one might believe—we recognize that the historical circumstances are completely changed, and we feel, often in a way that is not completely apparent to us, that today religion in our individual and social existence has a position and an importance that differs from what existed during the time of the crusades. Also for this reason, each of us is absolutely convinced that the attacks of September 11 are not matters of our conscience, of confession, of lived religious experience. But can we shape it into a religious fact for "the other side," for the terrorists who—I am thinking now of Palestine—blow themselves up wearing explosive vests, killing themselves along with ever-increasing numbers of other people, defenseless citizens not directly involved in any war? Such a picture of the fanatical religious terrorist is easy and convenient, and even has the appearance of wanting to "understand" the reasons behind actions that seem completely senseless to us. But this first outcome is precisely the one that confirms and solidifies the idea that here we face a clash of diverse cultures; and one need not say it of a secular and rational culture—ours—against a barbaric, primitive, and superstitious and in the end bloodthirsty culture and religion. Once such a representation of terrorism is accepted as valid, it is difficult to avoid the conclusion that this is a clash of diverse cultures, or even that this is the conflict between civilization itself and barbarism.

A similar error, precisely because what it suggests tends to appear obvious to us, forces us to look again at the origins, however remote, to which it returns. They are tied to the ambiguous relation between truth, authority, and power, which has characterized the Christian world since its beginnings. It is not at all obvious that the missionary spirit suggested by Jesus in the Gospels—"Go ye therefore, and teach all nations, baptizing them in the name of the Father" (Mt 28:19)—should naturally lead to the ideology of conquest that dominates modernity, the age of discovery, and the first colonization of the New World. It was a historically contingent development, which, on the contrary, was by now recognized and rejected explicitly by the churches—first among them the Catholic church—who were characterized by it and who really struggled to overcome all of the many and profound implications that still permeated many aspects of their doctrines and practices. Naturally, the idea that the truth revealed in Scripture and entrusted to the apostles should grant the Christian church the right to exercise a supreme authority over all the life of the human community is not born with colonialism and with the contemporaneous imposition of the absolute state in Europe. But it is reasonable to hypothesize that a carefully asserted and professed ideology, according to the Augustinian motto of *compelle intrare*, developed during this very epoch. The spirit of the crusaders, on the other hand, was still inspired by the idea of liberating the Holy Land and the tomb of Christ from the rule of the infidels. It was still a matter of territorial wars, for the most part. As confirmation, imagine that Saint Francis was thinking about taking a trip to a sultan in order to preach the Gospels and convert him, certainly not by forcefully imposing the Christian truth or by means of a Christianizing the state. Nevertheless, one can also recognize that the Franciscan spirit was not exactly the dominant one in the Christian Middle Ages. Alongside the real crusaders who were there to liberate the Holy Land, there were also the bloodthirsty crusaders, who more clearly had a "doctrinal" aim to get the heretics. One cannot, however, forget that the dangerous aspect of the heresies against which the medieval church engaged in bloody struggles was nevertheless for the most part political: these heresies became the object of persecution when, as happens rather often, they questioned the legitimacy of papal power, the riches of the church, and its defense of political authority.

Historians and philosophers of history (I am thinking of Wilhelm Dilthey, for example) have correctly brought to light the weight of the fact that, in the determination of the history of the church and of that same European theology and philosophy, the Christian church of the early centuries found itself the inheritor of many of the state functions once exercised by the Roman Empire, now in decline. As regards Dilthey's thesis—which I am here taking up in an autonomous way without any pretense of giving it a faithful reading—the strict relation between the defense of truth and the claim to political power would be encrusted on the Christian church, in a manner of speaking, from the outside, because it would find itself taking on the role of the Roman Empire after its fall. It is a thesis that circled widely in the Catholic debates of the nineteenth and twentieth centuries, and that at times was presented as the ideal of the end of the "Christian age"—what would have been the so-called donation of Constantine (which in truth never occurred), the origin of the temporal power of the popes and everything that follows. In many European nations such an end took place with the Protestant Reformation, which nevertheless (from the *cuius regio* of Luther to the dogmatic absolutism of Calvin) was never really liberated from its temporalistic prejudice; in other regions, I am thinking obviously of Italy, the problem of the temporal power of the popes would only be resolved with the end of the church state in 1870, without which, however, the claims of ecclesiastical authority would be placed on the laws and structures of the state (as one sees in an exemplary way even today in Italy).

The historical circumstances in which the connection between truth and authority arises can obviously be discussed at length; and even the hypothesis that sends us back, for Christianity, to the relation between the early church and the Roman Empire is absolutely not an exhaustive hypothesis, mainly because the question of the relation between truth and political power was posed to Christians long before they were called to inherit the structure of the empire, when the empire itself forced them, on pain of martyrdom, to bow to the cult of the emperor. In this way, the "sin" of the identification between truth and power would be turned against Rome, even though it had never imposed conversion upon its subjugated peoples through military force. Rémi Brague has correctly brought attention to the meaning of the Roman pantheon as an example of religious tolerance and pluralism.[3]

A component of the doctrinal absolutism that for many centuries characterized the attitude of the Christian churches, and that also, in Dilthey's hypothesis, is mixed with the question of the inheritance of the structures of the Roman Empire, is the metaphysical inheritance of Greek thought, so that, without completely developing here the discourse on this aspect of the question, one can perhaps say that the dissolution, the secularization, of this relation is really made possible in our world only when philosophy too has dealt with all of the consequences of the dissolution (also made possible above all by Christianity) of classical metaphysics of Greek origin. Moreover, precisely this Greek metaphysical inheritance also contains the premise for the identification of truth, authority, and political power: the *Republic* of Plato foresaw that the supreme authority of the state should be exercised by philosophers, that is, by those who had access to the ultimate truths.

What I hope to bring to light through these references, even though it might appear to the contrary, is the completely contingent—not "natural," as it would tend to appear—character of the connection between truth and power. In our cultural tradition, not only Christian but also classical and Greek, this connection has distant and therefore also deep roots. The link between political authority and some form of sacredness is not, however, an anthropological constant that one would discover in every human civilization, no matter how widespread it might be in the history of cultures. To consider this link as an anthropological constant is to consider democracy impossible; at best, the connection can appear to us as what in the Christian religion is called original sin. Certainly, it shows up continually in the history of individuals and societies; but it is not such that it blocks those very doctrines, such as the Christian one, from being understood as religions of redemption.

Let us summarize what has been said up to this point. If we become aware that we are no longer a society capable of waging religious wars, and if this does not at all seem to be a symptom of decadence or of immorality, but instead an element of the process of becoming civilized, we are also compelled to reconsider the obviousness of the idea that the enemy, the terrorist, the infidel, is motivated by pure religious fanaticism—only then are we perhaps in a position to understand that the connection between truth and power is not a necessary connection, but a contingent link bound to a group of historical circumstances. We Westerners—but perhaps also Islam and Judaism— are the inheritors of traditions in which, in fact, the political structures are constituted in close relation to the imposition of a religious faith. The idea that this link is a contingent one is not a statement of fact, proven as historical truth; but it is also not purely *wishful thinking*, as if we were to deliberately falsify the data of history and anthropology in order to console ourselves or in order to reach some end. It is rather—as happened to philosophical truths—a theory-praxis, a risky interpretation moved by a project, which is shown to be valid, in every case more valid than others, insofar as it is more capable of reading and developing our situation in a practicable direction. To recognize the truth-authority-power connection as an unavoidable anthropological constant would only mean—and many voices push us in this direction—preparing ourselves to conduct a new religious war by repeating a "naturalistic" scheme, so naturalistic that it would not make any sense to posit it as the basis for a conscious decision or a project of action. If we take on a project, it is because we consider that link to be contingent and modifiable. And, in terms of historical recognition, we also have good reasons for considering it in this way: the secularization of the modern world is, if not proof, a sign that one can move beyond the identification between a profession of a religious truth and an adherence to a strict political order.

In order to get rid of the misunderstandings, and the tragedies, of religious wars once and for all, we need to assert the projectual interpretation that I have proposed here and that, moreover, is the ethical-political sense of much of philosophy today. The pretense of authority by those who possess, or believe they possess, or claim to have discovered the truth—a truth—is merely a violence to which we are accustomed in a certain way, within a certain cultural and political tradition. The "missionary" and modern imperialistic sort of Christian universalism is an expression and, in fact, probably, the exemplary and "originary" manifestation of that pretense and of that violence, at least in our world. If we ask ourselves, very simply, who among us would consider it just, natural, human to compel someone by force to accept our faith, we might have some problematic answers: many of the formative relations with the smallest of us are grounded in a mix of violent imposition and emotive constriction (I fall for my lover and so on from there). Take the example of the aspiring suicide bomber whom I must, morally, try to stop, even against his will. Does the same go for those priests who baptize "pagans," primitives, and savages by force? All of this aside, even with babies the reliance on the force of punishments or on the power of affections is only a final resource, always preceded by the effort to try to understand, to explain, to appeal to one, albeit very imperfect, freedom. As in the case of hypocrisy, which is the tribute rendered by vice to virtue, here too the relation with the other is always represented as the relation to a freedom—a freedom that only in extreme cases, and without a theory that might positively justify it (thus it is also legitimate defense or all-out war), can resort to force.

◆ ◆ ◆

If it manages to divest itself of the violent characteristics that have been encrusted upon it as a result of the Western political tradition, Christian universalism can (re)discover its own authentic meaning, one that, moreover, was written in the text of the Gospels. Today this uncovering seems to be more pressing, and also more realizable, than in other ages. The churches have over time lost much of their "temporal" power, whether direct or "indirect," to determine consciences in a final way. Philosophy has parted ways from a rigidly objectivistic conception of truth by connecting it instead and ever more explicitly to the consensus of the community that shares paradigms, traditions, even prejudices, but that is aware of its own historicity. This seems to me to be an effect of the "Christianization"—even if it is not done on purpose—of that same philosophy today, in which one can speak of a dislocation of the very idea of truth toward the idea of charity, of respect, and of listening to the other. It is the very way of professing one's own religion and vision of the world that is changing profoundly, at least in the West, and not because we have become less faithful, more immoral, less religiously committed. The dialogue between the great religions up to now, which is spoken about often but occurs very rarely, is possible only if, within some of them, the faithful all feel compelled to believe in a less exclusive and less superstitious way. If I say, as I believe one should say, that since I believe that God became human, I can also think that, in other cultures, he became a sacred cow, an elephant, or a cat, I don't believe I am blaspheming; on the contrary, I believe that I am expressing a proper dimension of Christian truth.

A modern, secular, human rethinking of Christian universalism is possible on these grounds, and, if not in the ecclesiastical hierarchies then certainly in the community of believers, it is already fully underway. By developing this rethinking in all of its implications, we will also be able to defuse the bomb of religious wars. By beginning with no longer seeing the other as a religious fanatic completely prepared for the salvation of his soul, but, much more realistically, as someone who is struggling for concrete historical objectives, on which we can find an agreement, on the condition of not involving everyone in the costs of faith and the destiny of salvation. What from the Christian, but in general the "Western," point of view one can and one must do in order to depart from the mistakes of the war of religions is to begin living one's religiosity outside of the framework that is dear to Enlightenment rationalism, and that anticipates two possibilities: either the fanaticism of blind faith (I believe *quia absurdum*) or the skepticism of reason without roots and thus without an effective grip on the world. In reality, an attitude of rediscovered religiosity free from preoccupations with power and thus also free from every temptation of violent imposition ought to signify that the West today, rather than ready itself for an unending war to achieve the victory of its own "faith," seriously considers the historical reasons behind the clash with the so-called Third World. These reasons are economic—of inequality, of exploitation—and disguise themselves as reasons of faith and culture only for the self-interested ideological manipulation of those who possess wealth and power. Can we hope to find a similar spirit in the other participants in our dialogue, in our Muslim and Jewish friends? Much more than seeking a triumph of faith over others, the task that faces all of us is to rediscover, after the "metaphysical" age of absolutisms and the identity of truth and authority, the possibility of a postmodern religious experience in which the relation with the divine is no longer polluted by fear, violence, and superstition.

THE EVIL THAT IS NOT, 1

I f he thought he was making a prophesy, or even just expressing a hope, with the title *Beyond Good and Evil*, Nietzsche was certainly fooled. Today more than ever, above all in political language, good and evil (especially the latter) are omnipresent terms, imminent personifications of our fears and hopes. Not as adverbs,[1] which would perhaps be grammatically correct—such as in the common expressions "How is it going? Good, thanks, not bad"; or, "Today was a bad day"—but as substantives, as if one were dealing with rather precise beings to encourage or to fight. They were good times when "Evil" [*Il male*] could be used as the title of a satirical newspaper; today no one would ever think up such a title. Today, usually by carrying out—even in good faith—an ideological falsification, one speaks increasingly often of a struggle between good and evil, of an "evil empire" from which we must defend ourselves, that we will have to isolate and render harmless. This also occurs often by pointing out that whoever does not believe that the adverb refers to a noun has become an instrument of the devil, whose cunning consists precisely (like that of the mafia) in making one believe that he does not exist.

It is not easy to oppose the rampant belief in Evil with a more sober and demystifying attitude, one that by casting a little light might show that under the bed, or in history, there is no great Evil, but only dysfunction, problems, "evils" that should always be written in lower-case letters, so that one also does not become too comfortable in the convenient desperation of those who think that "there is no solution" and therefore it is useless to act. The unwavering force of the belief in Evil resides, however, in the harsh historical experience of the century just come to an end. It is too difficult to think that the concentration camps, the gulags, the massacres that continue in various regions of the world through wars, or those that "happen" because entire continents cannot afford drugs to fight malaria, AIDS, tuberculosis, and other infantile diseases—it is difficult to think that all of this is only "evil" in the sense that it does not go as we wish it would, because there is something that is "not working." It is this twentieth-century background—one that is also felt because, at the turn of the millennium, we all had to try to make sense of things—that warrants renewed attention by thinking and by philosophy to the question of "substantive" Evil.

Jean-Luc Nancy, in a short essay of extraordinary clarity and rigor (in a volume edited by Franco Rella), was right to propose a tripartition, theoretical and historical, of the concept of evil. Of the three ways that we can speak of evil—as misfortune, as illness, and as evil pure and simple—the first is characteristic of antiquity, upon which (one thinks of Oedipus) misfortune fell as a fatal event desired or permitted by the gods; the second is more specific to modern, rationalistic thought, for which there is in the world dysfunctions that disturb a fundamentally just order that one can and one must restore through appropriate actions. But today one can by now speak of evil only in a morally total and radical sense: the Nazi concentration camps are neither the misfortune that befell Oedipus nor an accident that disturbs the rational order of the world. "Absolute" evil has many senses, but they all have a metaphysical orientation; they are what lead us to rethink "substantive" evil, and to once again speak of an essentially tragic nature to humanity. The gulag and the lager are not only a past that we ought to and could try to forget. The tragic pessimism that snakes through our culture also has more recent motivations and more current justifications. That everything depends on the social division of labor and on exploitation—with the Marxist explanation having become impracticable (due to the failure of real socialism)—seems to many an inevitable consequence of the *hybris*, of the arrogance, characteristic of the technics (in fact, of the Technics) that dominate our globalized world.

A Jewish theologian whom I had the chance to hear speak many years ago (Professor Rubinstein, then a lecturer at Florida State University) proposed the paradoxical thesis according to which Hitler's extermination of entire populations would only anticipate the solution to a problem that, sooner or later, would be proposed even in more democratic countries: how to let go of the many people who are socially useless and who weigh heavily upon the scales of social welfare. . . . Unless, we could add, one thinks about AIDS, or the illnesses tied to "progress" (think of the cancers due to pollution), or the simple rise in sea level if, as seems likely, the polar icecaps are melting.

One cannot, faced with all of this, simply return to the modern faith in the possibility of therapeutic solutions. But is it then permissible to give ourselves over to cosmic pessimism? Or even to its easier and more popular version that accompanies a fierce defense of one's own interests to the point of desperation—what is often called realism or pragmatism?

Perhaps it is not helpful to respond in a definite way to this question; but it is not useless to rethink the concept of evil, its history and its implications, as many recent books invite us to do, motivated also by the urgency and radicality of our problems. A beautiful book by Rüdiger Safranski, which reconstructs—according to themes rather analogous to those found in Nancy's brief essay—the history of the concept of evil, suggests some theoretical outcomes worth considering. In the final pages of the book, Safranski takes his time discussing the Book of Job, the classic text on the theme of evil if there is one. As we know, at the end of his long "temptation" (born from a sort of wager between God and Satan), Job submits himself to the Lord, but not because he understood and accepted a rational explanation of his misfortunes. On the contrary, his submission does not have any basis, just as there was no basis—explanation, objective reason—for the actions of God that put him to the test. This total absence of grounds is also what one finds in the myth of Cain and Abel. Cain murders Abel out of envy; he is jealous of the fact that God favored Abel's offerings over his. This preference is also completely unexplainable and without explanation. In the New Testament there are also many similar pages: the parable of the workers who begin work late and yet receive the same pay as those who were working since the morning and who thus endure a type of "injustice" that can be attributed to the free choice of God; and Jesus's answer regarding the man born blind, whose misfortune derives neither from his own doing nor from the actions of his parents, but instead because it is pleasing to God. Certainly, the "God of the philosophers," the first, unmoved mover discussed in natural theology, could not be thought in these terms. As Luigi Pareyson, the great master from the University of Turin, taught us in his final works, human freedom and the very historicity of existence presuppose that God, as creator, is free and cannot be identified with a rational or necessary being. But for this reason one must also suppose that there is, or there was, what Pareyson called "the evil in God," for which the divine creation of the world was a victory over the negativity against which God himself nonetheless had to settle accounts.

Yet Pareyson's argument, which takes up themes already present in Jakob Boehme and in Schelling, cannot really be utilized, as one often does today, to support a tragic vision of existence and the idea that Evil is a substantive reality. We are speaking of evil only because we have to explain freedom, and not the other way around. Pareyson also says that evil is nothing other than the abyss—the inexplicability—of freedom. In much of contemporary philosophy this gives rise to an emphasis on the notion of responsibility: what human beings do in history does not realize some preordered plan, or some eternal law, but is completely tied to their choices, which can find a criterion and a guiding thread only in their attentiveness to "values," that is, to the choices already tested that we have inherited and we receive from those like us. But is it possible to conceive this freedom radically without discovering, as Job did, that in the final analysis there is nothing more than what the Gospels call "Grace"?[2]

14

THE EVIL THAT IS NOT, 2

Can we, without any irreverence, and in fact with total awareness and respect, apply a sentence from Bonhoeffer to evil? That sentence states that "Einen got, den es gibt, gibt es nicht" (a God that is is not). And so one could say "Ein Böse, das es gibt, gibt as nicht" (an evil that is is not). It would not only be a way to sum up much of the traditional speculation on evil—from Saint Augustine forward—but also a thesis perfectly in line with the "destruction of ontology" initiated by Heidegger, which constitutes one of the most important, and most intimately religious, outcomes of twentieth-century philosophy.

One could even show that the destruction of ontology about which Heidegger speaks—or even his thesis according to which Being is not identified with beings, and thus is nothing "objective" but always the light in which any objectivity can appear—is a direct consequence of the traditional reflection on the problem of the "reality" of evil. It is precisely in the case of evil, as it is, moreover, in the case of God, that the insufficiency of the notion of Being that Heidegger calls "metaphysics" is revealed, and this makes it coincide with a form of objective existence, "given" as definitive, necessary, and thus within reason's grasp. When we struggle to say that God is, or exists, we do not know well what this really means: certainly not that God "gives itself," *es gibt,* as being that could be encountered in space-time, as with an object that appears in our normal experience. Philosophical atheism in all ages has always had a good time demonstrating the absurdity of the "existence of God" conceived in these terms. Furthermore, this God of the philosophers, as Pascal already said, has nothing to do with the God of Abraham, of Isaac and Jacob, and with Jesus the God incarnate.

As in the case of the "existence of God," it is precisely Jesus who renders superfluous both the metaphysical notion of divinity and, by that count, the thesis of atheism (since to demonstrate that the God of the philosophers does not exist does not in any way matter to the truth of the Gospels)—thus the debate over the reality or nonreality of evil can be overcome only by the Christian message of resurrection. The thesis that I proposed at the beginning, namely, that "an evil that is is not," is simply a translation of the sentence from Saint Paul: "O death, where is your victory?"[1]

I will clarify:

1. The metaphysical disputes over the reality or nonreality of evil have never really been able to resolve the problem they have addressed. Nothing that exists can be called evil: either because, from a religious perspective, it is a creation of God, or, even without reference to God, because it appears impossible not to identify the good with being itself. This impossibility of thinking evil uncovers the insufficiency of the ontological categories transmitted to us by metaphysics. Heidegger, moreover, began his reflection against the metaphysical idea of being by reflecting on the problem of freedom and predestination: if true being, namely, divine being, were really the pure act or the necessary being of metaphysics, and thus the God of the philosophers, we would not be able to think our existence as Being—because we are history, freedom, hope, everything but unchanging and necessary reality.

2. Within the framework of the metaphysical conception of Being— for which it is really only what "gives itself" [si dá] in an unchanging,

rationally necessary, demonstrable, "scientifically" ascertained form—one can think of neither God, nor Jesus, nor the history of our existence, nor even evil. All of these "realities" that we also experience and that appear undeniable to us "are" not in this metaphysical sense. But if being is not the objective "self-giving," what will it be? One could respond with a line from Bernanos (which ends his *The Diary of a Country Priest*): "Everything is grace." In philosophical terms I would say with Heidegger that being, if it is anything, is event, *Ereignis*. Certainly, *es gibt Sein*: but only in the sense that *es, das Sein, gibt*. Being gives, this is its only thinkable "essence." I am not proposing simply to leap outside of philosophical language in order to pass over to the language of Christian revelation. What I am saying is that the same philosophy—at least in the form that appears to me as the most capable of corresponding to our age and our specific historical vocation—must return to the Christian message in order to resolve the contradictions and aporias of metaphysics.

3. In the perspective of Being as gift and event there is no evil. But with this, the discourse does not come to an end; on the contrary, it is just beginning. How do we explain to ourselves the undeniable experience of evil? Social injustice, the extermination of whole groups, our very individual awareness of being in some way "guilty" (or, according to an emblematic page of the Gospels, the problem of the man born blind)?[2]

4. For (my-our) philosophy—therefore not according to a doctrine that pretends to be definitive and metaphysically necessary—evil today is first and foremost metaphysics itself, the identification of being with its self-giving [*darsi*] as unchanging object, the confusion of the God of Jesus with the God of the philosophers. Evil is the wild mastery of measurable objectivity, the anxiety over not losing this control, in all of the many senses in which we have experiences of it, from the pretense of not losing the physical good looks that allow us to seduce, to enjoy, to prevail over others, to the will to power of the great historical individuals, to the multiple forms in which the principle of service develops on all levels of our experience.

5. But why the reference to Saint Paul and to the sentence "O death where is your victory?" The metaphysical confusion of being with the unchanging and immutable givenness (*Gegebenheit*) of the object makes it impossible to think of death and to accept it as "natural." The highest crime that we know of is taking another's life, murder. Anyone who is born is always exposed to dying a "natural" death. From here emerges the traditional problem, also metaphysical, of theodicy. If one also, and most often, dies "naturally," it seems it would be the fault of God, an act that we have to "justify." Biblical revelation, however, does not offer any pretext to a metaphysically satisfying theodicy. Neither the adventure of Job nor the scene in the Gospels with the man born blind provides "explanations" for evil. In both of these cases, it seems, on the contrary, that the error, the evil itself, consists in wanting to find an explanation that does not exist. Reason, it seems, would be considered satisfied if it were able to grab on to some "objective" law on the basis of which the disasters suffered by Job or the blindness of the innocent man might end up being well deserved. Instead, what the Scriptures ask us to do in these two cases is to accept these events as "grace"—and thus pleasing to God.

◆ ◆ ◆

If we change the terms of Bonhoeffer's sentence about the "God that is (not)" and we translate it into the second in which even "evil is not," and this becomes the keystone of an ontology of the event (for which even "a Being that is is not" but happens), then the sentence from Bernanos that was cited above, "everything is grace," simply becomes "everything is history"—and that means gift, and thus *geben* (everything is given, everything is a "self-giving"; Wittgenstein: the world is everything that is the case, *was der Fall ist*). The revolt against metaphysics initiated by Heidegger is the beginning of a post-Nietzschean thinking that not only is similar to the fruit of a philosophical excogitation, but belongs to the world of the happening of being in the age of accomplished nihi-lism. It is the age in which *es mit dem Sein selbst nichts (mehr) ist*—there is nothing (more) to Being itself. The breakup of Eurocentrism, the dis-solution of the idea of history as a single course of events whose center has always been considered that of human-European civilization: an event of (our) being, or simply the event of being that concerns us in our existence and our historical situation. One knows that Foucault coined the phrase "ontology of actuality," even if with much less onto-logical emphasis than one ought to have. For him the expression only indicated a thinking that reflects on the specific historical existence of the person philosophizing, such that one could instead use the expres-sion "anthropology of actuality." Foucault was perhaps already beyond structuralism, but his aim still remained unflinchingly descriptive. It is only through a radical reading of Heidegger—that which I have let myself call a "leftist" reading of Heideggerianism—that the ontology of actuality becomes the only conceivable ontology; and as it is not descriptive, neither contemplative nor aesthetic (one might read Hei-degger's review of Jaspers's *Psychologie der Weltanschauungen* in Hei-degger's *Pathmarks*), it is practically engaged in the event itself that it makes an effort to "grasp." In the end, we are here faced with a radical historicism, for which it *is* only what happens, and the happening is the result of the response that existing being gives to messages that they receive from their *Geschick*, from the whole of what is sent to them and what in its turn is none other than the result of other happenings of the same type. The problem of understanding the call in *Sein und Zeit* to "the anticipatory resoluteness for one's own death" is resolved only by interpreting it as a call to the radical historicity of human existence: every one of us is only a mortal being that inherits and transforms the traces of other mortal beings—and Being is only the crystallization of this inheriting-interpreting-transforming-handing down. Even the expression of Benedetto Croce according to which history is (only) the history of the freedom that must be read, beyond some Hegelian meta-physical residues that still seem to weigh it down (is Spirit "something" that has history? or is it nothing other than history?), assumes a full sense only if we think about it within the framework of the Heideggerian ontology of Being as event, and so that the thesis of Marx on Feuerbach, the famous one according to which the philosophers must transform the world and not simply interpret it, no longer takes on a metaphysical or positivistic sense if it is understood in light of the Heideggerian notion of the event that is always necessarily interpretation and transformation, namely, authentic praxis.

WEAK THOUGHT, THOUGHT OF THE WEAK

C an the silence of the defeated discussed by Benjamin in his "Theses on the History of Philosophy" be placed alongside the silence (of Being) that Heidegger recommends we listen to beyond and on the background of the voices of the beings that question us from every quarter? In the case of Heidegger, the relevant texts are far too numerous to allow them to be cited in any specific way. But it is a comparison that merits being developed—not for reasons of pure Heideggerian philology, but rather in view of a return to Heidegger in terms of the ontology of actuality, even beyond the limits to which weak thought has thus far been pushed. I believe the first step on this path must be the dialogue with the Japanese Count Kuki that takes up a large part of *On the Way to Language*. Here silence is discussed at length, and especially in the final pages, where one supposes there ought to be an authentic silencing of silence. There is no doubt that these pages put forward, and not just at first glance, a mystifying Heidegger. And yet up to a certain point, if one does not forget the beginning of the dialogue, one of the difficulties that resonates most clearly as an obstacle to the mutual understanding of the two interlocutors can be traced back to the "Europeanization of man and of the earth," what tends to disappear in the obviousness of the dominion of "reason" and is instead the root of the drying up "of everything that is essential."[1]

Now, the dominion of reason, which has been imposed since the time of the Enlightenment, determines our language as it rests "on the metaphysical distinction between sensuous and suprasensuous" of sound and script, on the one hand, and signification and sense, on the other. From this starting point, one arrives at Benjamin's defeated without too much difficulty if one thinks about the motives that—from the beginning, from *Sein und Zeit*—inspire Heidegger's polemic against metaphysics, and if one does not forget that what Heidegger points out as its characteristic traits are the very same that Nietzsche would identify: the opposition of sensuous and suprasensuous, of sound and signification. Benjamin's defeated are silenced by metaphysics because this is the basis of the technological-scientific rationalization of the earth, what to the Heidegger of *Sein und Zeit* appears to be the evil to fight by trying to recover some memory (of the forgetting) of Being. One can also observe well that Heidegger never turned this conception of metaphysics-technics into an explicit principle of social critique, as happened to other authors who matured in the same atmosphere of existentialism and the avant-garde during the early part of the twentieth century. That is not to deny that this originary practico-political inspiration of the refusal of metaphysics is a constant undercurrent in the work of Heidegger, and is rediscovered, with outcomes that we certainly do not share, in his support of Nazism in 1933. The same *Kehre*, the much discussed turn in his thinking during the 1930s, of which he speaks in the "Letter on Humanism," can only be understood as the recognition that the authenticity (*Eigentlichkeit*) Heidegger discusses in *Sein und Zeit* only makes sense in relation to an event (*Ereignis*) that is not an individual matter but rather has the characteristics of a revolution. Proof of all of this is found in the pages of *Zur Sache des Denkens*.[2] They are pages in which one can find a proximity of Heidegger to Marx, one that is not shocking if one thinks precisely of the reasons that inspire his critique of metaphysics since *Sein und Zeit*—when Heidegger, in these pages from the 1960s, identifies the task of thinking as not being satisfied with the everyday presenting of what is present ("die vorhandene Gegenwärtigung des Anwesenden"[3] seems to echo the famous words of Brecht "Because things are the way they are, things will not stay the way they are," and above all seems to share many traits of the "school of suspicion" of Marx, Nietzsche, Freud). The point is, obviously, to establish if and at what point that horizon of *alétheia* that we cannot forget in favor of what is simply present might also after some time be able to move itself closer to Marxist, dialectic concreteness, to that totality without which the particular truths are always ideological falsifications inspired by the opacity of particular interests. For this we have only some indication from Heidegger, in particular if we place the beginning of the dialogue with Count Kuki in relation to the conclusion of the lecture from 1964. Here, Heidegger asks himself yet again why our experience of truth today is "naturally" oriented to be conceived as correspondence, *orthotes*. That which happens is what is unthought, presence as such and the opening (*Lichtung*) that makes it possible (*gewaehrende*). The why of this situation remains hidden. The *Lichtung* is not only the opening of presence, but the opening of presence concealing itself, "Lichtung des sichverbergenden Bergens."[4] Trying to grasp presence as such, however, risks its loss in a "grundlose Mystik," in a "schlechte Mythologie," and thus in a "verderblicher Irrationalismus."[5] But rationalism and irrationalism are already terms that let themselves be determined according to *ratio* as calculation, as the technical rationalization of the world of causes and effects. Here, it seems to me, we return to the opening pages of the discussion with Count Kuki. Even in a manner fundamentally inspired by *Sein und Zeit*: the refusal of metaphysics as the ideology of the world of *totale Verwaltung*.

This initial, and constant, inspiration from Heidegger is above all what is recalled in what I proposed to define "weak thought." What was born as a Nietzschean-Heideggerian reading of the situation is, in the same period (the end of the 1970s and onward), described by Lyotard as the postmodern condition. In my perspective, which does not differ from that of many other Italian philosophers of the last generation,[6] the multiplication of the specialized languages of science, which moreover also reflects the social phenomenon of the division and specification of the different spheres of existence already described by Max Weber, exhibits a tendency of modern society and culture to be moved in the direction of "the loss of the center," which Nietzsche pointed out as the very meaning of nihilism (man rolls away from the center toward X). According to a perspective that among other things inspired Heidegger's essay "The Age of the World Picture" (1938), this was the very meaning of the completion and end of metaphysics: the impossibility of enclosing the world within a unified picture, of describing it with one rational language. Heidegger also saw this fragmenting of every unity as the symptom of nihilism. Yet he never defined himself as a nihilist, as Nietzsche had done (who thought himself to be the first accomplished nihilist). This reluctance on the part of Heidegger to consider nihilism as the true "destiny" of Being, and not only as the extreme point of danger (but "where danger is, there grows the saving power also," a line from Hölderlin that Heidegger often cited), probably depends on the same reasons that maintain his effort to remember Being in terms not very far from that risk of mystical irrationalism that he noted in the pages of the lecture from 1964. As readers of his work know, Heidegger in the 1930s lived through an experience of "turning," the famous *Kehre* of the "Letter on Humanism." Its meaning is that authenticity, *Eigentlichkeit*, about which he speaks often in *Sein und Zeit*, cannot be thought as the result of an individual *metanoia*, what would be identified with the "explicit self-projecting for one's own death" that seemed, at the time, the motto for a clearly pessimistic existentialism, but that already in that same *Sein und Zeit* was perhaps a call to position oneself consciously in one's own historical situation (remember the famous line according to which "Dasein chooses its own heroes"). The turn takes note that even language that struggles to go beyond objectifying metaphysics fails to meet its goal because it is not a tool at the disposal of humanity, but something to which humanity is disposed: we are on a level where there is not just humanity, as the Sartre of *Existentialism Is a Humanism* wanted, but where there is, first and foremost, Being. One can summarize the meaning of the Heideg-gerian *Kehre* as a journey from *Eigentlichkeit* to *Ereignis*. To remember Being does not mean ascetically conquering one's own authenticity through the anticipatory resoluteness for death, but listening to the meaning of Being that is given in the event, in the age, in the world. (Let us remember that in the 1930s Heidegger began to speak of the world in historical and plural terms, as is seen in the essay "The Ori-gin of the Work of Art.") This listening, however, will be developed in the writings that come after the 1930s—except in the courses and essay on Nietzsche—above all as the listening to the poets and to the inaugural words of the tradition. Biographically, one remembers the tragic error that led Heidegger to support Hitler in 1933—the exclu-sive attention to the poets and to the most ancient (and auratic) words of the metaphysical tradition is probably explained with the desire to keep himself at a distance (after that error) from politics, in which he also, in a passage from the essay on the work of art, had recognized (as in philosophy, religion, and ethics) a capacity to act as the site where truth is set to work. But it is precisely this prevalent orientation toward the auratic nature of the words of the pre-Socratics and toward what is uncovered, by revealing in the poetry that which justifies the impression—much more than an impression, in many of Heidegger's readers—that he had not been substantially capable of defeating the risk of mystical irrationalism that he clearly recognized in the lecture from 1964. Weak thought is born from considerations like these. It is a matter of pushing, or pulling, Heidegger in the direction of the "urban-ization" that was already attempted by Gadamer with his hermeneutic ontology. Weak thought presents itself as something more radical. It thinks that nihilism is not only the greatest risk for Being, but its "authentic" destiny, that of dissolving it as "objective" foundation. The lecture from 1964 I am recalling speaks of "das Sein als Grund fahren lassen"—letting go of Being as Ground. But to whom and why does such a "dissolution" or weakening of Being as stable, objective, unwav-ering foundation really appear as a risk?

Obviously, nihilism is a risk for metaphysics. As we know, however, metaphysics must be overcome, or at least no longer pursued, because it is the basis for the technical world of total organization. Therefore, the same worry that Heidegger had about being identified with Nietzsche the nihilist is very likely the sign of a persistent nostalgia for metaphysics, of his inability to "let go of Being as foundation." The expression of that same nostalgia can appear, and in fact did appear, in his insistence upon listening to the silence. What would be an authentic saying of language? "An authentic silencing of silence," Heidegger writes in *On the Way to Language*. One can refuse to call it mysticism, but certainly it is something quite similar to what Heidegger himself stigmatizes.

The problem that weak thought tries to resolve in its own manner is also that of remembering Being in a way that does not end up as mysticism. It is not only a question of the interpretation of Heidegger; or, at least, it is also a question that concerns the presence of his thought in contemporary culture. For example, doesn't a certain mannerism that seems to follow Derrida, and that often ends up a sophisticated game of interpretations that are more like creative literature than critical discourse, have something to do with this problem of how to rethink Being? Ultimately, if it is not the exhaustive and exhausting listening to the auratic words of ancient thinkers and of poets, what is it?

One needs to recall Heidegger's original motivations. Why does he try to leave metaphysics behind? Certainly not to have an "idea" of Being that better corresponds to its true essence. We do not need any fundamental ontology, at least if understood in this way. We rebel against metaphysics because in it we recognize the basis of the total organization of the world within which we ourselves could no longer call Being. And metaphysics, with its practical-political cost of total organization, is what "silences" the horizon of *alétheia*, and does not let us hear the silence on whose background alone the words of everydayness can stand out and be rendered audible—not necessarily in-authentic in themselves, but in-authentic if they are not "positioned" (*Erörtern*, again from *On the Way to Language*) in relation to the opening that makes them possible. Heidegger maintains in the lecture from 1964 that the nonlistening to the silence of *alétheia* is not at all a natural given. As *alétheia* is an unveiling that has the character of an event, thus even the not letting be heard of its silence is "event." It happens that metaphysics makes us forget the ontological horizon that makes beings and the intraworldly commerce with them possible. The silence that we ought to manage to listen to by escaping from the effect of the oblivion produced by metaphysical "noise" is the result of a silencing. Here we are saying that, although Heidegger never confronted the problem of violence thematically—and in fact lets us think, coherently in all of his works, that violence is metaphysics itself, the forgetting of Being in favor of beings (from here begins anything that could be called a Heidegger-inspired "ethics")—the only possible nonessentialistic and nonmetaphysical definition of violence we can successfully think beginning from his thought is precisely the silencing, the peremptoriness: of first principles, of Being that would be given "objectively" by leaving Dasein only the possibility of exclaiming "eureka" and of feeling reassured, but also threatened, by its overwhelming power.

With these considerations in mind, how are we to think about listening to the silence in a way that avoids the risk of mysticism? If metaphysics is the silencing of everything that does not reenter into the intraworldly game of the concatenations of cause and effect, object of manipulation and of calculation, we can nevertheless ask ourselves—in order to avoid falling into that very mysticism of the irrational—who is silencing whom. The return to Benjamin, certainly not authorized explicitly in any of Heidegger's texts, and not even by his political positioning, does not, however, seem unjustified. The silence that one must know to listen to is not a vague mystical background that would be evoked by some demonic character from the world of technology and calculating reason. It is very true that Heidegger was never compelled to indicate technology as the expression of the capitalistic mastery of society, but certainly he was not ignoring Max Weber and his idea of modern rationalization as both the effect and the cause of the spirit of capitalism's coming into its own. The silence (even here) of Heidegger on these connections, which he could not run away from, can in our view be attributed to the decision to distance himself from politics after the error and the delusion of the choice for Nazism. But these are themes belonging to (abbot?) Farías, although for us it is not at all a question of being faithful to the explicit intentions of the author. We are guided by the intention of the work itself, beginning from *Sein und Zeit* and from the impossibility of reading the antimetaphysical polemic already underway in this book as a "theoretical" need for fundamental ontology. We can only explain *Sein und Zeit* as the way that Heidegger corresponded to the demands of the spirit of the avant-garde in the 1910s and 1920s, which was trying (even in the debates between the natural sciences and the human sciences) to find a way to resist the universal homogenization and the transformation of society in the giant productive machine that would be the object, not much later, of Chaplin's satire *Modern Times* and of the Frankfurt School's Hegelian-Marxist critiques. The silence that metaphysics keeps us from listening to is nothing other than, let us say it again, the silence of the defeated that Benjamin discusses in his "Theses on the History of Philosophy." Where Benjamin insists on showing that revolutionaries are "nourished by the image of enslaved ancestors rather than that of liberated grandchildren," we can do no less than recall the Heideggerian conception of nonmetaphysical thinking as *An-denken*, remembrance that is also gratitude and *pietas*. Listening to the silence of the defeated is not at all a historicistic expedient for constructing a more complete and "true" picture of the past. Benjamin speaks of it rather in terms of a "dance of tigers" that makes the *continuum* of history leap by grasping a moment of the past as charged with a sort of eschatological present. Even here, how could we not remember the authentically lived temporality that has always been at the heart of Heidegger?

Certainly, we are always left with the problem of explaining why Heidegger never followed the path, inspired by him, that we now believe we must take. Why didn't he more explicitly connect metaphysics and violence, not only in the form of the forgetting of Being but above all in the form, much less "mystical," of social domination? Moreover, not even we can defend the definitive value of this reading of his work. We stand under a different constellation; but, precisely because we do not believe this has anything to do with the eternal Being of metaphysics, we do not feel like relativists. It is rather that we are called by a different appeal that is certainly Being, but in its self-giving in the event.

16 FROM DIALOGUE TO CONFLICT

Why from dialogue to conflict? Isn't hermeneutics—that philosophical orientation from which, on the heels of Pareyson and of Gadamer, and before them Heidegger and Nietzsche, I always sought inspiration—precisely a philosophy of dialogue? Years ago, due also to the experience of American debates where hermeneutics had become simply a name for all "continental" philosophy (from Habermas to Foucault, to Derrida and Deleuze) by replacing existentialism and phenomenology, I had proposed to speak of hermeneutics as the new *koiné*, the new shared idiom for a large part of contemporary philosophy. This diffusion, so to speak, of hermeneutics has also fatally "diluted" it, as I observed in some of my books and essays from the 1990s. Against this dilution—which reminded me a bit of the "light" interpretation of Nietzsche's eternal return given by Zarathustra's animals ("everything goes, everything returns, the wheel of being eternally turns," there is nothing for us to worry about)—I at that time thought of opposing a more forceful accentuation of the unavoidable nihilistic outcome of hermeneutics that is taken seriously. That every experience of truth is interpretation is not for its part a descriptive or metaphysical thesis; it is an interpretation that does not legitimate itself by pretending to show things as they are—on the contrary, one cannot at all think that things, or Being, "are" in some way;

interpretation and things, and Being, are all part of the same historical happening; even the stability of mathematical concepts or of scientific truths is a happening; propositions are verified or falsified always and only within paradigms that for their part are not eternal, but qualified according to their time period. I was speaking of the nihilistic outcome of hermeneutics, taking up the term from Nietzsche but with a Heideggerian inflection; as we know, for Heidegger Being is event, the very opening of those horizons that Kuhn calls paradigms. To the Heideggerian notion of the event I added—I believe always faithful to his teaching—a more explicit philosophy of the history of Being, with Nietzschean origins; if we look at the history of Being as it is given and gives itself to us in the West (citizens of the *Abendland*, the land of the evening), the more reasonable reading we can give of it is the one proposed by Nietzsche with his idea of nihilism: history in the course of which, as Heidegger summarizes, there is nothing more to Being itself. Exactly, of Being as such: the *on he on* of Aristotle, Being as unchanging structure that stands beyond every contingency and guarantees the immutable truth of every true, that has the "destiny" of walking without end toward the no-longer-being Being as such. Following Nietzsche, I saw this process as the guiding thread of the development of Western culture, from truth as the contemplation of the ideas in Plato to the "subjective" foundation of the true in Descartes and Kant, all the way to the positivistic identification of truth with the result of an experiment constructed by the scientist and also to the very "universalization" of hermeneutics, well beyond the human sciences, in theories like that of Thomas Kuhn.

This outline is too simple, as historians of philosophy point out—always the friends-enemies of the theoretical. But it is one that Nietzsche and Heidegger share with Dilthey, even with Husserl and, more distantly, with Hegel; and it is one needed to make a theoretical that would not be metaphysical—for if one denies the overly simplistic schematization of the history from which we come and in which as interpreters we seek out our legitimization, we can only claim to have to reflect an objective order that will inevitably have to be thought as subject to historical events. I am remembering here that, notwithstanding all of his claims to construct the way out of Nietzschean nihilism (from which it has to be distinguished due precisely to its radical proximity), Heidegger is still the author of sentences like "das Sein als Grund fahren lassen" (*Zur Sache des Denkens*) and "Sein—nicht Seiendes—'gibt es' nur."[1] And that from the other side, in my work from recent years, the "simple" schema of Western history as nihilism is also inspired by the notion of secularization seen as the progressive realization of that *kenosis* of the divine that is the essence of Christianity.

Here then is the sense of the nihilistic outcome of hermeneutics. That does not mean that there are no longer criteria for truth, but only that these criteria are historical and not metaphysical, certainly not tied to the ideal of "demonstration," but rather oriented toward persuasion—truth is a matter of rhetoric, of shared acceptance, as is the case even for the scientific proposition, which has value insofar as it is verified by others, by the scientific community, and nothing more.

However, once again, why from dialogue to conflict? It is by now clear that when one says that truth is a matter of persuasion, dialogue plays a central role. Heidegger often quotes the verses of Hölderlin: "Many of the heavenly ones he has named . . . since we have been a conversation [*Gespräch*]."[2] A Heideggerian "logic" can only think truth as the result of dialogue and nothing more. The conclusion is not that we are in agreement because we have discovered (there outside) truth, but rather, we say that we have found truth when we are in agreement. Therefore, at the root of truth as event (not reflection and the like) there is the plurality of interpreters and their agreement or disagreement. Here I encounter once again one of the elements of the teachings of Luigi Pareyson, namely, the idea that interpretation can fail. This idea has always somewhat limited my sharing of Gadamer's theory of the "fusion of horizons" and in general of hermeneutic dialogue. As if in that theory there were too much optimism, too much irenicism. This sort of trait even announces itself in Habermas's theory of communicative action. In his hands argumentative dialogue always has the air of being an affair between transcendental subjects, between researchers in a laboratory. The limits that they encounter are still their subjective limits, their possible opacity, even when it is produced by unfavorable social conditions (exploitation, exclusion) that Habermas certainly did not intend to accept. Or it is even a matter simply of not confusing different types of argumentation, as in the case of Wittgenstein's linguistic games—with the saints in church and the like. Ever since he moved toward a gradually more explicit treatment of Kantianism in the place of his origins in critical Marxism, Habermas has spent less time on the ways that the conditions of a dialogue are realized. That is confirmed, it seems to me, by the fact that his political positions are accentuated by a sort of "institutionalism," a faith barely justified in the international organizations such as the United Nations, whose inability to hinder the will of the strong countries (of the strong country) is by now doubted by few of us.

I can confess without difficulty that I have become sensitive to this problem—which I summarize in the title "From Dialogue to Conflict"—for reasons that do not have in fact anything to do with questions regarding theory, but that instead are all too clearly tied to what, with an expression from Hegel's aesthetics, I would somewhat pompously call the "general condition of the world." One is first aware of this through the feeling of annoyance that provokes us more insistently and clearly with every call to dialogue. Not only in recent Italian politics, where the contenders argue by reprimanding one another for not wanting to engage in dialogue, without ever naming the "thing itself" and with results that would be comical if it were not a matter of the country's destiny. In truth, if we reflect on the reasons behind our impatience with the rhetoric of dialogue, we realize that we are only expressing a much broader and, if I can say, philosophically relevant revolt—namely, the revolt against the ideological "neutralization" that by now rules everywhere in the culture of the First World, of the industrialized West. It is a matter of what is often called *pensée unique*, which in the final analysis is identified by what politicians call—when they name it—the *Washington consensus*, outside of which there is nothing but terrorism with all of its derivatives. Put in this way, it is clear that it seems like a caricature. But it has the advantage of showing without ambiguity an increasingly apparent trait of our contemporary existence. That this is a philosophically relevant matter can be denied only by whoever thinks of philosophy as the cultivation of languages and problems completely outside of everyday existence. Naturally, even the person who sees things in this way is convinced of the "absolute" relevance of what it does, in the very name of that metaphysical conception of Being that pictures it as the fundamental structure of the real, to which it is useful to "entrust" oneself in order to reach salvation. But without examining the good reasons of those who—like Heidegger, Nietzsche, and much of contemporary philosophy—think that one needs to be saved from metaphysics itself, because it is the product and support of the relations of domination. The *pensée unique* in which we are immersed has the value of making us understand—in many ways in our bones—that metaphysical objectivism, today above all declined as the power of science and technology, is nothing other than the most up-to-date (and most elusive) form of the domination of classes, groups, and individuals. Neutralization and the power of every type of expert are the same thing. It is the experience that, even within the small horizon of Italian society, we have when we see the disappearance of the differences between Right and Left. A disappearance that, moreover, is widespread, at least in the Western world of capitalistic rationality, as this latter idea is always most visibly irrational and manifests its purely predatory essence without any shame.

Can we fans of Heidegger finally redeem his antimodernism, his distrust for universal, technological scientific mastery? Everything, or almost everything, for which he has long been reprimanded as a sign of his Black Forest obscurantism, of nostalgia for the patriarchal life of the German countryside, or even, we are saying, of his unfortunate choice of Nazism in 1933 takes on a different hue in light of what is happening today due to globalization and the imperialistic homogenization of the planet. The Heidegger who took Hitler's side in 1933 did something that we could certainly never condone. But thinkers like Lukács and Bloch did the same by choosing the communism of Stalin. In both cases, whatever might be our preference for the one or the other of the two positions, it is a matter of deciding upon a historical commitment that both the one and the others see as philosophically determining, but not—at least for Heidegger—as responding to a metaphysically universal value. I want to say that in the case of Heidegger it was a consciously "sided" choice, understood as corresponding to a specific destiny, that of the German people, the destiny that is, on the contrary, seen as the call of Being, but exactly of a Being that announces itself only as a particular historical sending, within the limits of a situation (the prevailing power of capitalistic America and Stalinist Russia) that is also unreadable—in its perspective—in terms of universal values and essences. In many aspects, it was "sided," but not in the name of claimed universal values, the choice of Lukács and Bloch, who instead confided in a global rationality of history in which the revolutionary proletariat, with whom they believed they were siding by choosing Soviet communism, was the agent of the redemption of all humanity. I know that this point, Heidegger's choice in the 1930s (which I see as very similar, however diametrically opposed in term of content, to the choices made by big figures such as Lukács and Bloch), raises delicate questions, and I invoke it here certainly without the intention of being provocative. Yet perhaps they are the same thing: to the objectivistic, metaphysical, technological-scientific neutralization that characterizes *pensée unique* also belongs the good conscience with which the industrial West feels itself to be the bearer of "true" human rights, of the just political order (to the point of wanting to impose it, or of wanting to make itself to believe it has imposed it, even with wars against other populations), of the authentic civilization that conforms to the nature of man. Heidegger teaches us to reject all of this as the survival of metaphysics, namely, of mastery, even with his tragic error in 1933. An error that appears to us as an error not because we feel that we are representatives of the true humanity only the West could deliver. Rather, we correspond, or we intend to co-respond, to an alternative historical call that in many ways is analogous to what Heidegger claimed to hear not only in his support of Nazism in 1933, but above all when, beginning with his essay "The Origin of the Work of Art" (1936), he began to elaborate a concept of the event of Being that, by having to think of it as freedom, novelty, and project, and not simply as the development of a metaphysical essence given once and for all, also found him faced with its tendency toward conflict. What happens in Heidegger's thought after the "turn" of the 1930s and that continues to provoke us today is as much the "mystery of the iniquity" of his support of Hitler as it is his awareness that one cannot speak of authenticity, *Eigentlichkeit* (the big word in *Sein und Zeit*), except within the *Ereignis*; translated: you cannot become authentic through a simple, individual moral decision; it is a matter that concerns Being itself, as he also says in the "Letter on Humanism" directed at Sartre. But must we simply stand still and wait? Even at the risk of making a mistake and betraying certain fundamental aspects of his own philosophy, Heidegger thinks he has redeemed himself: for and against something, without any metaphysical pretense of sovereign neutrality in the name of a philosophical access to first principles and universal values. "Wer gross denkt, muss gross irren," as he repeated often in the years that followed. He who thinks great thoughts also makes great errors.

I referred to the essay on the work of art because it is there that he sought out the connection between the happening of truth and conflict. I will repeat briefly the passages implicit in what was said up to this point (will I also think *gross*, with the linked inevitability of the *irren*?). Truth, if it is not the reflection of an eternally given order of essences and structures, is happening, and dialogical happening ("Since we have been a conversation," with Hölderlin). Truth gives itself when we agree. But will dialogue really always be so peaceful? Platonic faith, which is found again in Gadamer, in his creativity, always supposes that there is, somewhere, the true. And that someone knows about it a bit more than the others: the slave who in the Socratic dialogue manages to discover truths of geometry is guided by someone who conveniently questions him. As it might be with the Socratic-Platonic dialogue, it is certain that today's rhetoric of dialogue has many aspects that make it seem a mask of mastery—and for this we in fact endure in our growing annoyance toward it. Now, in the essay on the work of art that I am referring to here, Heidegger defines the work of art as "truth setting itself to work." And the reading of this definition interprets it correctly as the affirmation of the "inaugural" character of the work. What Heidegger seems to be thinking about is that since the truth of a proposition can be proven by someone only within a historical paradigm, which is not simply the articulation of an eternal structure (the nature of man, first principles, and the like) but happens, is born, has an origin (analogously to the paradigms of Kuhn), the site of this happening is sought in the work of art. We can consider Dante's *Divine Comedy*, Shakespeare, Homer, and in fact the Bible inaugural in this sense. In the same essay, while slowly developing the idea of the work as the place where truth happens as the opening of a historical horizon, the birth of a language, and so on, Heidegger also notes other ways that truth happens beyond the work of art—which he does not, however, discuss in greater depth and which he ultimately leaves outside of the horizon of the writings that follow, as they are always oriented toward finding the event of truth in poetry or in the originary wisdom of the sayings of the pre-Socratics. What constitutes the basis of the inaugural force of the work of art, and this today seems to me more important than it appeared to me in the past, is the fact that it keeps the conflict between world and earth open. Without repeating here the analyses discussed elsewhere, the first, world, is understood as the articulated horizon, the paradigm, that the work inaugurates and within which it "dwells"; the other, earth, is understood as that reserve of always ulterior significations that, as the term itself indicates, are tied to life—the life of nature and of the person—and that constitute an obscure ring from which originates the impetus to project, to change, to become something other. Existence, Heidegger thinks, is project: and Being itself, by giving itself only through humanity, its "shepherd" or even lieutenant, is event as novelty, indeducibility, happening pure and simple, not necessary but always inaugural. The history of Being, moreover, that in Heidegger is the problematic linking of openings, of paradigms, is possible because there is "earth," namely, the succession of generations: it is to this rhythm—remember the saying from Anaximander—that the paradigms, the openings, the events of Being leave their place to the ones that follow.

But the earthliness does not let itself be enclosed within the stability of a happy dialogue, which would establish truth as the harmonious birth of a new opening. The events of the avant-garde of the twentieth century, which Heidegger certainly lived, show how much the power of "disorientation" (Heidegger, not only Benjamin, speaks of *shock* as the effect of the work) is contained in the birth of an alternative opening, even in that "innocent" realm of art. The happening of truth "disturbs." The transition from one paradigm to the other—remember that the example used most often by Kuhn is the abandoning of the Ptolemaic model in favor of the Copernican one—does not occur through a "dialogue," but rather through the character of a "catastrophic" change that is only allowed to be rationalized *après-coup*. As far as one makes the effort to adapt to a new rational conception of history, one cannot not see that the great transformations, which certainly do not occur in a single moment, are never the effect of rational decisions, and even less of "democratic" ones. In order to establish democracy in Iraq, Bush taught us, with all of his generals, that one needs an act of force. And moreover the French revolutionaries—the official beginning of the contemporary age according to textbooks—did not decide to behead the king through a referendum. To begin from constitutions, first and foremost those democratic ones, it is always a matter of "events" that are not "logical," but rather discontinuous in relation to what preceded them, and therefore also not dia-logical. Rational argumentation is certainly preferable, and no one doubts that on this point Habermas and Rawls are correct. But the institution of a horizon of argumentativity, at least for now (and we must emphasize it, against every irrationalism based on metaphysical or fundamental irrationalism), involves a battle, a conflict, perhaps that which, according to Marx, must happen in order to exit from prehistory.

The "for now" is here not only a rhetorical expression. The unfortunate choice, the tragic error of Heidegger in 1933, has value to us as an example because it seems to recognize in the present situation traits analogous to those that he had to deal with. As then, we are in a condition of "urgency," with the impending threat of the loss of freedom. If, luckily, we can also resist looking for too many analogies, the concrete differences are numerous, the reference to that age matters to us only as a reminder of the fact that philosophy, if it does not want to be metaphysics (which is always just defending things as they are), must look at the general condition of the world and allow itself to be questioned by it. To think of it already in this way, however, places it in the necessity of being committed. One cannot try to leave metaphysics behind—objective, defensive, "realistic"—without being involved in the conflict from which alone the truth-event can originate. Freedom—the human projectuality in which only Being announces itself as such—is always threatened by metaphysics (that is, by the violence of mastery). During the time of Heidegger's turn, he was threatened by the closing grasp of capitalistic imperialism, Stalinist communism, and German Nazism. Today the threat is constituted by the neutralizing forces of globalization in which mastery is hidden under the mask of economic rationality and techno-science seen as the only hope for "progress" and for "peace." Our situation is, in certain ways, more insidious, even if infinitely more comfortable than that of the 1930s. The silencing of every tendency toward conflict—which then was certainly far more explicit—realizes that condition Heidegger criticized in the passage from Plato that makes up the exergue of *Being and Time*: not only do we not have a response to the question of the meaning of Being, but we are also forgetful of, we are forgetting, the very question itself. For this reason, trying to remember Being means nothing other than, for us today, taking a stand against neutralization, taking a side. With whom and for what is not terribly difficult to establish, without letting ourselves be too affected by many who today, correctly even if always with metaphysically arrogant reasons ("we are the true defenders of humanity" and so on), believe they must throw away Heidegger's ontology because of his error in 1933. Making the effort to remember Being as projectuality and freedom clearly means choosing to stand with those who project more because they possess less: the old Marxist proletariat. It is not the metaphysical holder of the truth because it is free to see the world outside of ideology; rather, it is the bearer of generative essence because more than any other individual, group, or class, it is defined by a project and is wholly projected toward the transformation of its own condition—that is, authentically *ex-sisting*.

NOTES

INTRODUCTION

1. Naturally, the full picture of this issue is very complex and almost constitutes a chapter unto itself in the history of twentieth-century philosophy, at least since the end of the Second World War. The "Farías case" was provoked by Victor Farías's volume *Heidegger and Nazism* (Philadelphia: Temple University Press, 1991), published in France in 1987, and more recently was fueled by *Heidegger y su herencia: Los neonazis, el neofascismo europeo y el fundamentalismo islamico* (Madrid: Tecnos Editorial S, 2009). Against it, it seems, there is at least François Fédier, *Heidegger: Anatomie d'un scandale* (Paris: R. Laffont, 1988), and the more balanced judgment that emerges, for example, in the volume edited by Jürg Altwegg, *Die Heidegger Kontroverse* (Frankfurt: Athenäum, 1988). For a complete (and subdued) outline of the issue, well beyond the limits of the Heideggerian tradition, the take offered by Richard Bernstein, *The New Constellation: Ethical-Political Horizons of Modernity/Postmodernity* (Cambridge, Mass.: MIT Press, 1992), 79–141, continues to be useful.

2. [Translator's note: Vattimo makes many references throughout this book to Heidegger's famous *Es gibt Sein*, which he translates into Italian with the impersonal verb *darsi*. The best rendering of *darsi* in English is perhaps "to be the case" or "it happens that ..." But it is important to note that the literal meaning of *gibt* as

"it gives" is maintained in *darsi*, which is in its reflexive form a self-giving or presentation—thus, I have opted to use "give" as the basis for my translation of this concept, noting the places where it is meant in the sense of *es gibt* and *darsi*.]

3. On the problem of origin in Heidegger, an essential contribution in the direction that I am setting forth here is without a doubt the work of Reiner Schürmann. As we know, Schürmann addressed the theme of the originary within a context that dealt with the political implications of Heidegger's discourse (and biography). And he does it by showing that the Heideggerian interests can be resolved neither in the painstaking research of the beginning of Greek thought, nor in a defense of the "new beginning" in the Führer's Germany. See, in particular, Reiner Schürmann, *Heidegger on Being and Acting: From Principles to Anarchy* (Bloomington: Indiana University Press, 1987), 33–43. On this, and on Schürmann in general, see Alberto Martinengo, *Introduzione a Reiner Schürmann* (Rome: Meltemi, 2008), 45–51.

4. Schürmann, *Heidegger on Being and Acting.*

1. THE NIETZSCHE EFFECT

1. Broadly speaking, Dominque Janicaud, *Phenomenology and the "Theological Turn": The French Debate* (New York: Fordham University Press, 2001).

2. I am thinking, for example, of Massimo Cacciari in the 1970s: see *Krisis: Saggio sulla crisi sul pensiero negative da Nietzsche a Wittgenstein* (Milan: Feltrinelli, 1976); and *Pensiero negative* (Venice: Marsilio, 1977).

3. For my interpretation of Nietzsche I refer the reader to *Il soggetto e la maschera* (Milan: Bompiani, 1974); and to the collection *Dialogue with Nietzsche*, trans. William McCuaig (New York: Columbia University Press, 2008).

4. It is, once again, the point of departure for my position contained in *Beyond Interpretation: The Meaning of Hermeneutics for Philosophy*, trans. D. Webb (Cambridge: Polity, 1997).

5. It is actually the content of a note from 1886–87, which begins with "Against Positivism," in Friedrich Nietzsche, *Writings from the Late Notebooks*, ed. R. Bittner (Cambridge: Cambridge University Press, 2003), Notebook 7 [60]: 139. [Translator's note: I have deviated from the English translation of Nietzsche's text cited above in order to remain consistent with Vattimo's use of this passage in other works.]

6. Hans-Georg Gadamer, *Truth and Method*, 2nd rev. ed., trans. J. Weinsheimer and D. Marshall (New York: Crossroad, 1992), 474.

7. A reading of this sort, which to me seems the most coherent, requires that in the Italian translation of the sentence one inserts two commas, after "Being" and after "understood"; the commas are there in the original German but are required only because of grammatical rules that are in place for relative clauses. I discuss all of this in "Storia di una virgola," *Iride* 23 (2000): 323–34.

8. See H.-G. Gadamer, *Reason in the Age of Science*, trans. Frederick G. Lawrence (Cambridge, Mass.: MIT Press, 1981); see also various pages of *Truth and Method* cited in "Storia di una virgola."

9. Friedrich Hölderlin, "Versöhnender, der du nimmer geglaubt . . . ," *Sämtliche Werke*, ed. Friedrich Beissner, Groß Stuttgarter Ausg., vol. 2 (Stuttgart: W. Kohlhammer, 1951), 137, line 50.

10. Friedrich Nietzsche, *Twilight of the Idols*, in *The Anti-Christ, Ecce Homo, Twilight of the Idols, and Other Writings*, trans. Judith Norman, ed. Aaron Ridley and Judith Norman (Cambridge: Cambridge University Press, 2005), 171.

11. See Friedrich Nietzsche, *The Birth of Tragedy, and Other Writings*, trans. Roland Speirs (Cambridge: Cambridge University Press), 139–53.

12. On the meaning of Nietzsche's perspectivism I have taken important suggestions from Jürgen Habermas, *Knowledge and Human Interests*, trans. Jeremy J. Shapiro (Toronto: Beacon, 1971), 290 et passim.

13. I proposed this hypothesis in an essay from 1987, which appeared in English a year later: "Hermeneutics as *Koiné*," *Theory, Culture and Society* 5 (1988): 7–17.

14. Even if it would be difficult to call Rorty's neopragmatism "naturalistic." See Richard Rorty, *Philosophy and the Mirror of Nature* (Princeton: Princeton University Press, 1979). He claims, moreover, to inspire McDowell, who is referenced below.

15. Normal science, in the language of Thomas Kuhn, is "research firmly based upon one or more past scientific achievements, achievements that some particular scientific community acknowledges for a time as supplying the foundation for its further practice." Kuhn, *The Structure of Scientific Revolutions*, 3rd ed. (Chicago: University of Chicago Press, 1996), 10. These accepted outcomes and their related methods support what Kuhn calls a paradigm. On the other hand, one calls "revolutionary" science that which develops out of the invention of a new paradigm. See ibid., 92.

16. John McDowell, *Mind and World* (Cambridge, Mass.: Harvard University Press, 1994).

17. Ibid., 23.

18. Ibid., 14.

19. Ibid., 16.

20. Gareth Evans, *The Varieties of Reference* (Oxford: Clarendon, 1982).

21. McDowell, *Mind and World*, 19.

22. On all of the discussions and relative documents I refer the reader to the long introduction by R. Dottori to H.-G. Gadamer, *Verita e metodo 2: Integrazioni* (Milan: Bompiani, 1996).

23. For Heidegger, as we know, to think—*Denken*—is also and above all to recollect—*An-denken*—to listen to the history of Being as it is inscribed within language.

24. Ronald Giere, *Scientific Perspectivism* (Chicago: University of Chicago Press, 2006).

25. Friedrich Nietzsche, *Thus Spoke Zarathustra*, trans. A. P. Del Caro (New York: Cambridge University Press, 2006), 173–78.

26. For more, see Vattimo, *Il Soggetto e la maschera*.

27. Friedrich Nietzsche, *Human, All Too Human*, trans. R. J. Hollingdale (New York: Cambridge University Press, 1996), section 57, p. 42.

28. Friedrich Nietzsche, *The Gay Science*, trans. Josefine Nauckhoff and Adrian Del Caro, ed. Bernard Williams (Cambridge: Cambridge University Press, 2001), section 354, pp. 211–14.

29. Friedrich Nietzsche, *On the Genealogy of Morality*, trans. Maudemarie Clark and Alan J. Swensen (Indianapolis: Hackett, 1998).

30. Nietzsche, *The Gay Science*, section 50, p. 62.
31. Ibid., section 343, p. 199.
32. Nietzsche, *Human, All Too Human*, section 34, p. 29.

2. THE HEIDEGGER EFFECT

1. Martin Heidegger, *Sein und Zeit* (Tübingen: Niemeyer, 2001). English translation: Heidegger, *Being and Time*, trans. J. Macquarrie and E. Robinson (San Francisco: Harper, 1962).
2. It makes up volume 9, edited by F. W. von Herrmann.
3. In Martin Heidegger, *Pathmarks*, ed. W. McNeill (Cambridge: Cambridge University Press, 1998), 1, where he cites Jaspers.
4. Here too is a literal citation from Jaspers: ibid., 2.
5. Ibid., 3.
6. Martin Heidegger, *The Phenomenology of Religious Life*, trans. M. Fritisch and J. A. Gossetti-Ferencei (Bloomington: Indiana University Press, 2004), 7.
7. Heidegger, *Pathmarks*, 20.
8. Heidegger, *The Phenomenology of Religious Life*.
9. Ibid., 30, translation modified.
10. Cited from R. Cristin, ed., *Fenomenologia: Storia di un dissidio* (Milan: Unicolpi, 1999), 59.
11. E. Bloch, *Geist der Utopie* (Frankfurt: Suhrkamp, 1985). English translation: Block, *The Spirit of Utopia*, trans. A. Nassar (Stanford: Stanford University Press, 2000).
12. *Antrittsrede*, in *Jahresheft der Heidelberger Akademie der Wissenschaften*, 1957–58:20–21.
13. See Heidegger, *Being and Time*, 264: "That which has been uncovered and disclosed stands in a mode in which it has been disguised and closed off by idle talk, curiosity, and ambiguity. Being towards entities has not been extinguished, but [author's note: however not on the contrary, and nevertheless] it has been uprooted."
14. Ibid., 265.
15. Martin Heidegger, *Was ist Metaphysik?* (Frankfurt: Klostermann, 1949).

16. Heidegger, *Sein und Zeit*, 230.
17. Heidegger, *Being and Time*, 272.
18. The passage is cited and discussed in G. Semerari's preface to E. Husserl, *La filosofia come scienza rigorosa* (Bari: Laterza, 1994), xi–xii.
19. Section 76 of *Being and Time* (448–49) confirms the presence of Nietzsche in Heidegger's reflection on history. The proposal of Zarathustra to cast off the stone of the past that weighs upon his shoulders, and that inspires the Nietzschean idea of the eternal return of the same, is certainly one of the important references for Heidegger.
20. Heidegger, *Being and Time*, 268–70.
21. See John McDowell, *Mind and World* (Cambridge, Mass.: Harvard University Press, 1994), 24–28.
22. The reference is obviously to the division between Right and Left that one sees in the Hegelian school.
23. For the reference to Nietzsche I always point the reader to my *Nietzsche: An Introduction* (Stanford: Stanford University Press, 2002); and *Dialogue with Nietzsche* (New York: Columbia University Press, 2000).
24. Martin Heidegger, *Nietzsche*, vol. 2, *The Eternal Recurrence of the Same* (New York: HarperCollins, 1991), 338.

3. THE AGE OF THE WORLD PICTURE

1. Martin Heidegger, "Die Zeit des Weltbildes," in *Holzwege* (Frankfurt: Klostermann, 1950); English translation: Heidegger, "The Age of the World Picture," in *Off the Beaten Track*, ed. and trans. J. Young and K. Haynes (Cambridge: Cambridge University Press, 2002), 57–85.
2. I am thinking of philosophers like Paul Feyerabend, Nelson Goodman, Hilary Putnam and his "internal realism," Bas van Fraassen. One can find brief yet precise outlines of their positions in the relative entries of the Garzantina di Filosofia.
3. On these topics I refer the reader to the excellent work of V. Crupi, "Scienza, ontologia, metafisica: Heidegger and I nomi della filosofia," *Iride* 28, no. 3:627–44; and see also "Tematizzazione e matematizzazione," *Filosofia* 51, no. 2:251–77.

4. Martin Heidegger, *Was heißt Denken?* (Tübingen: Niemeyer, 1954); English translation: Heidegger, *What Is Called Thinking?*, trans. J. G. Gray (New York: Harper and Row, 1968).

5. Martin Heidegger, *Being and Time*, trans. J. Macquarrie and E. Robinson (San Francisco: Harper, 1962), 272.

6. James Joyce, *A Portrait of the Artist as a Young Man* (New York: Penguin, 2003), 184.

7. Martin Heidegger, *Pathmarks*, ed. W. McNeill (Cambridge: Cambridge University Press, 1998).

8. Martin Heidegger, *Gesamtausgabe* (Frankfurt: Klostermann, 1983), 25:25–26.

9. Heidegger, *Pathmarks*, 95.

10. Ibid., 83.

11. Might the fact that science functions, even when practiced "inauthentically," be attributable to the claimed "scorn" the existentialistic Heidegger had for average everydayness, for which even this sort of science would be sufficient? As in Croce, only an "economic" matter? But then, the scientific opening would be identified simply with the banality of the "they"—and also the average opinion particular to that age? Or would the science practiced by the existentially "authentic" scientist be only that which does not claim to be the only source of the truth of things? Paradoxically, if the truth were neutral objectivity, perhaps this claim would be legitimate. This too. But, once again, here we will always be only in the manner of the hurdy-gurdy song of Zarathustra's animals, or in the manner of a tolerant conception of the plurality of linguistic games, of the versions or redescriptions of the world. The plurality, here, does not create problems because it always seems that it might be supposed that the world is nevertheless firmly one; games, versions, redescriptions are exactly *only* games, versions, and so on.

12. On the disappearance of the term and of the theme of "authenticity" in the so-called second Heidegger, and its "reduction" to the event, I refer the reader again to my work on Heidegger, especially Vattimo, *Essere, storia, e linguaggio in Heidegger* (Genoa: Marietti, 1989).

13. See John Richardson, *Existential Epistemology: A Heideggerian Critique of the Cartesian Project* (Oxford: Clarendon Press, 1986).

14. Heidegger, *Pathmarks*, 91.
15. See ibid., 286.
16. See Heidegger, "The Age of the World Picture."

4. THE TEMPTATION OF REALISM

1. Hilary Putnam, *Reason, Truth and History* (Cambridge: Cambridge University Press, 1981), 49–50.
2. Ibid., 49.
3. In an interview conducted by Mario De Caro and published in *La Repubblica* on September 24, 2011, Putnam claims that in recent years he has tried to overcome both "metaphysical realism" (for which "reality is describable in a unique way, a way that establishes definitively our ontology") and "internal realism" through a "realism of commons sense," according to which there are "many correct descriptions of reality." De Caro—moreover as one might expect from a newspaper article—is satisfied a bit too easily with this answer, anxious not to place Putnam among the "realists" à la Searle. Realism, here, seems to be identified only with the opposite of empirical realism—that is, with the thesis according to which there is something outside of us and the subject does not create all of that which he understands. Poor Kant and the poor hermeneuticians, these latter the certain polemical target of realists à la Searle, might give thanks; moreover, they never dreamed of siding with Berkeley. See also Putnam, *Renewing Philosophy* (Cambridge, Mass.: Harvard University Press, 1992).

5. TARSKI AND THE QUOTATION MARKS

1. Richard Rorty and Pascal Engel, *What's the Use of Truth?*, trans. William McCuaig (New York: Columbia University Press, 2007).
2. For example, Diego Marconi, *Per la verità: Relativismo e filosofia* (Turin: Einaudi, 2007).
3. Ibid.

6. BEYOND PHENOMENOLOGY

1. Walter Benjamin, "Theses on the Philosophy of History," in *Illuminations*, trans. Harry Zohn (New York: Harcourt Brace Jovanovich, 1968), 260.
2. See Martin Heidegger, *What Is Called Thinking?*, trans. J. G. Gray (New York: Harper and Row, 1968), 36. Other passages about Being turning itself toward us are cited and discussed in Gianni Vattimo, *Essere, storia e linguaggio in Heidegger* (Genoa: Marietta 1989).
3. Here I am thinking of the reading of the *Krisis* offered by Enzo Paci, *The Function of the Sciences and the Meaning of Man* (Evanston, Ill.: Northwestern University Press, 1972).
4. On November 17, 2004, President George W. Bush awarded John Searle the National Humanities Medal: see www.neh.gov/news/archive/20041117.html.
5. W. V. O. Quine, "On What There Is," *Review of Metaphysics* 2 (1948).
6. Here the reference is to the eleventh thesis in Marx, "Theses on Feuerbach," in *Collected Works of Karl Marx and Friedrich Engels, 1845–47*, vol. 5, *Theses on Feuerbach, The German Ideology and Related Manuscripts* (New York: International Publishers, 1976).

7. BEING AND EVENT

1. It is the motto of Paul Feyerabend's methodological anarchism. See Feyerabend, *Against Method*, 4th ed. (London: Verso, 2010).
2. Karl Otto Apel has rightly spoken of a semanticization of Kantianism; see Apel, *Comunita e comunicazione* (Turin: Rosenberg e Sellier, 1977).
3. For example, Martin Heidegger, *Pathmarks*, ed. W. McNeill (Cambridge: Cambridge University Press, 1998), 54.
4. See Jürgen Habermas, *Theory of Communicative Action*, vol. 1 (Boston: Beacon, 1985).
5. See Martin Heidegger, *Beiträge zur Philosophie (vom Ereignis)* (Frankfurt: Klostermann, 2003), especially sections 50, 54, and 60. I am translating it liberally as "absence of emergency," as have

the American translators P. Emad and K. Maly, who in their turn also translate the term as "lack of distress." See Martin Heidegger, *Contributions to Philosophy (From Enowning)* (Bloomington: Indiana University Press, 1999). R. Polt on the other hand reads it as a constant term in his excellent study *The Emergency of Being* (Ithaca: Cornell University Press, 2006). Even the importance taken on today by the idea of the event seems to me conditioned by the situation in which we live, and in which it seems like nothing can happen.

6. See Edmund Husserl, *Teleologie in der Philosophiegeschichte*, in *Die Krisis der europäischen Wissenschaften und die transzendentale Phänomenologie: Ergänzungsband: Texte aus dem Nachlass, 1934–1937*, Husserliana 29, ed. R. N. Smid (Dordrecht: Kluwer Academic, 1993), 410–11.

8. THE ETHICAL DISSOLUTION OF REALITY

1. In the original German: *"Es mit dem Sein selbst nichts mehr ist"*: Martin Heidegger, *Nietzsche*, vol. 4, ed. David Farrell Krell (San Francisco: Harper Collins, 1991), 201.

2. See Gianni Vattimo, *Dialogue with Nietzsche*, trans. William McCuaig (New York: Columbia University Press, 2006), 181–89.

9. METAPHYSICS AND VIOLENCE: A QUESTION OF METHOD

This translation was originally published in *Weakening Philosophy: Essays in Honour of Gianni Vattimo*, ed. Santiago Zabala (Montréal: McGill-Queen's University Press, 2007), 400–21.

1. See Dieter Henrich, "Was ist Metaphysik—Was ist Moderne? Thesen gegen J. Habermas," *Merkur* 442 (1986): 495–508, which discusses Habermas, "Rückkehr zur Metaphysik: Eine Tendenz der deutschen Philosophie?," *Merkur* 39 (1985): 898–905.

2. See Donald Davidson, "On the Very Idea of a Conceptual Scheme," in *Inquiries Into Truth and Interpretation* (Oxford: Clarendon, 1984).

3. Henrich, "Was ist Metaphysik."

4. See, for example, note 10/168 in the Colli-Montinari edition, and *On the Genealogy of Morality*, Second Treatise, section 16.

5. It is note 40/21 in the Colli-Montinari edition.

6. Friedrich Nietzsche, *Daybreak: Thoughts on the Prejudices of Morality*, trans. R. J. Hollingdale (Cambridge: Cambridge University Press, 1997), 220n547.

7. See, for example, Friedrich Nietzsche, *The Gay Science*, aphorism 329; and Gianni Vattimo, *Il soggetto e la maschera* (Milan: Bompiani, 1974), 116ff.

8. See A. Janik and S. Toulmin, *Wittgenstein's Vienna* (New York: Simon and Schuster, 1973).

9. As G. Carchia writes in *La legittimazione dell'arte* (Naples: Guida, 1982), 123.

10. Emmanuel Levinas, *Totality and Infinity: An Essay on Exteriority*, trans. Alphonso Lingis (Pittsburgh: Duquesne University Press, 1969).

11. Martin Heidegger, *What Is Called Thinking?*, trans. J. G. Gray (New York: Harper Perennial, 1976).

12. On this, refer to Gianni Vattimo, *Essere, storia e linguaggio in Heidegger* (Genoa: Marietti, 1989), chap. 4.

13. On the history of metaphysics as the history of various first principles assumed over time as foundation, see Reiner Schürmann, *Heidegger on Being and Acting: From Principles to Anarchy* (Bloomington: Indiana University Press, 1987).

14. Martin Heidegger, *Nietzsche*, vol. 4, ed. David Farrell Krell (San Francisco: Harper Collins, 1991), 201.

15. See Martin Heidegger, *Identity and Difference*, trans. J. Stambaugh (Chicago: University of Chicago Press, 2002), 37: "The event of appropriation is that realm, vibrating within itself, through which man and Being reach each other in their nature, achieve their active nature by losing those qualities with which metaphysics has endowed them."

16. I am thinking of the chapter on the "ontological need" in Theodor W. Adorno, *Negative Dialectics* (New York: Continuum, 2000).

17. See ibid., 68.

18. Heidegger, *Identity and Difference*.

19. See ibid. The "qualities" (*Bestimmungen*) that metaphysics has endowed to humanity and Being are nevertheless those of subject and object, as appears in the same pages of *Identity and Difference* that speak of the reciprocal *Herausforderung* in which humanity and Being, in the epoch of metaphysics, are coinvolved.

20. See Martin Heidegger, *On the Way to Language* (New York: Harper and Row, 1971).

21. As Heidegger advises in *Zur Sache des Denkens*.

22. See the accurate observations by Dieter Henrich about Habermas's "Rousseauianism" in Henrich, "Was ist Metaphysik," 503–4.

23. On this, see also Gianni Vattimo, *The Transparent Society*, trans. D. Webb (Baltimore: Johns Hopkins University Press, 1992), chap. 1.

24. In a sense that Heidegger did not consider explicitly, but that can be connected to his conclusions in the essay "The Age of the World Picture," in *Off the Beaten Track* (Cambridge: Cambridge University Press, 2002).

25. Richard Rorty, "The Priority of Democracy to Philosophy," in *Objectivity, Relativism and Truth: Philosophical Papers*, vol. 1 (Cambridge: Cambridge University Press, 1991).

10. FROM HEIDEGGER TO MARX: HERMENEUTICS AS THE PHILOSOPHY OF PRAXIS

1. Here let us also remember the title of a beautiful book on Heidegger: Reiner Schürmann, *Heidegger on Being and Acting: From Principles to Anarchy* (Bloomington: Indiana University Press, 1987).

2. See S. Latouche, *L'invention de l'économie* (Paris: Albin Michel, 2005).

11. THE END OF PHILOSOPHY IN THE AGE OF DEMOCRACY

1. "The world is everything that is the case," in Ludwig Wittgenstein, *Tractatus Logico-Philosophicus* (Routledge: London, 1992), 1.1.

2. "Die vorhandene Gegenwärtigung des Anwesenden," in Martin Heidegger, *Zur Sache des Denkens* (Tübingen: Niemeyer, 1969), 79. English translation: Heidegger, *On Time and Being*, trans. Joan Stambaugh (Chicago: University of Chicago Press, 2002), 71.
3. "Grundlose Mystik, schlechte Mythologie, verderblicher Irrationalismus," in Heidegger, *Zur Sache des Denkens*, 79; *On Time and Being*, 71.

12. TRUE AND FALSE UNIVERSALISM

1. Aphorism 82 in *The Wanderer and His Shadow*.
2. Richard Rorty, "Solidarity or Objectivity?," in *Objectivity, Relativism, and Truth* (Cambridge: Cambridge University Press, 1991).
3. See Rémi Brague, *Europe: La voie romaine* (Paris: Criterion, 1992).

13. THE EVIL THAT IS NOT, 1

1. [Translator's note: the overlap between adverb and substantive is much clearer in the Italian language (*bene* and *il bene*, *male* and *il male*).]
2. For further reading: K. Bhasin, S. Kothari, and B. Thapar, eds., *Il teatro del bene e del male: Riflessioni critiche dopo l'11 settembre* (Turin: Gruppo Abele, 2002); Franco Rella, ed., *Il male: Scritture sul male e sul dolore* (Bologna: Pendragon, 2001); Tzvetan Todorov, *Memory as a Remedy for Evil* (Chicago: Seagull Books, 2010); Rüdiger Safranski, *Das Böse: Oder das Drama der Freiheit* (Frankfurt: Fischer, 1999); Luigi Pareyson, *Ontologia della libertà* (Turin: Einaudi, 1995).

14. THE EVIL THAT IS NOT, 2

1. 1 Corinthians 15:55.
2. John 9:1–41.

15. WEAK THOUGHT, THOUGHT OF THE WEAK

1. See Martin Heidegger, *On the Way to Language* (New York: Harper and Row, 1971), 4 and 16.
2. See the lecture "Das Ende der Philosophie und die Aufgabe des Denkens" of 1964, in Martin Heidegger, *Zur Sache des Denkens* (Tübingen: Niemeyer, 1967), 97.
3. Heidegger, *Zur Sache des Denkens*, 79; English translation: "The End of Philosophy and the Task of Thinking," in *On Time and Being*, trans. Joan Stambaugh (New York: Harper and Row, 1972), 71.
4. Heidegger, "The End of Philosophy and the Task of Thinking," 78–79.
5. Ibid., 79.
6. I am thinking above all of essays collected in the volume edited by Aldo Giorgio Gargani titled *Crisi della ragione* (Turin: Einaudi, 1979).

16. FROM DIALOGUE TO CONFLICT

1. Martin Heidegger, *Sein und Zeit* (Tübingen: Niemeyer, 2001), section 44.
2. The reference is from Heidegger's reading of Hölderlin's unfinished poem "Conciliator" in the essay "Hölderlin and the Essence of Poetry." See Martin Heidegger, *Elucidations of Hölderlin's Poetry*, trans. Keith Hoeller (Amherst, N.Y.: Prometheus Books, 2000).

INDEX